THE WOMEN WERE THERE

Love Jane xx

THE WOMEN WERE THERE

Nineteen women who enlivened
Australia's history

NANCE DONKIN

Collins Dove
Melbourne Australia

Published by COLLINS DOVE
60–64 Railway Road, Blackburn Victoria 3130
Telephone (03) 877 1333

© Copyright Nance Donkin 1988
All rights reserved. Except as provided for under Australian copyright law, no part of this book may be reproduced without permission in writing from the publishers.

Cover design by Mary Goodburn
Designed by Noni Edmunds
Typeset in Atlantic by Solo Typesetting, South Australia
Printed by The Book Printer, Victoria

National Library of Australia
Cataloguing-in-Publication data:

Donkin, Nance.
  The women were there.

  Bibliography.
  Includes index.
  ISBN 0 85924 647 7.

  1. Women—Australia—Biography. 2. Women pioneers—Australia—Biography. 3. Australia—History. I. Title.

994'.0088042

Front Cover: Jane Penelope Atkinson
            daughter of Mary Reibey

CONTENTS

Marriage — Colonial Style	1
Esther and Jane	9
The Captain's Wife — Elizabeth Macarthur	17
Anna Josepha — First Lady	29
Girl on a Horse — Mary Reibey	39
'Lik a Ladey'	49
Letters From Women	61
A Woman of Letters	71
The Elegant Misses Macleay	81
A Passionate Australian — Annabella Boswell	91
A Five-pound Future	101
Lady Jane — An Independent Spirit	111
Women on the Goldfields	121
Women in the West I. Georgiana Molloy	131
Women in the West II. The Busy Bussells	145
Daughters of the Rectory	155
The Ladies Bo-peep	169
Mary McConnel, Queensland Pioneer	179
Harriet Daly of Darwin	189
Reference Notes	199

ACKNOWLEDGEMENTS

The publishers wish to thank the following for granting permission to reproduce photographic material.

The Mitchell Library, State Library of NSW for the photographs of Jane P. Atkinson, Elizabeth Macarthur, Anna J. King, Mary Reibey, Margaret Catchpole, Mrs Alexander Macleay, Rachel Henning; State Library of Tasmania for photographs of Louisa Ann Meredith, Lady Jane Franklin; The Hastings District Historical Society for photograph of Annabella Boswell; A. V. R. Bunbury, Marybrook, W.A., for photograph of Georgiana Molloy; Mrs E. Vines of *Cattle Chosen*, Busselton, W.A. for photograph of Bussell family; Oxley Library for photograph of Mary and David McConnel; State Library of South Australia for photograph of Dominic and Harriet Daly.

While every care has been taken to trace and acknowledge copyright, the author tenders apology for any accidental infringement where copyright has proved untraceable.

PREFACE

As far back as Australia was inhabited, women were there with the men. For the Aboriginal tribes who lived on and with the land for many many thousands of years, men may have been the great hunters but women were the food-gatherers, diggers of roots, collectors of shellfish and plant foods, trappers of small game, child-minders, and educators by example; occupying a lowly but essential place.

In January 1788 when the First Fleet came with its strange cargo and European settlement began, the lonely land was changed for ever. Again women were there with the men, again theirs was a lowly but essential role. This book tells the stories of a small number of the Anglo-Celtic women—some Ladies and Others—who would help to reshape the country's future.

Early records are not always reliable. Names had different spellings, were sometimes changed for compelling personal reasons; dates were confused; people who could neither read nor write were not good witnesses and their human recorders often were little better. So dates and figures and statistics vary and the same woman can be written down as being 15 years of age, as 17, and the next year, 20. But the past of women in Australia is fascinating territory which we are just beginning to discover, and rich soil indeed for the writer/digger.

Nance Donkin

*Sweet Sue and Black-eyed Poll
saying goodbye to their loved ones*

MARRIAGE — COLONIAL STYLE

The intense quiet was unnatural; trees were unrecognisable. The heat was alarming; the weather, like everything else in that unknown place, was out of kilter, summer heat in late January instead of winter snow or sleet. Nothing was familiar to the senses, not the shape of a hill or the smell of wet grass or soot from chimneys. There *were* no chimneys, for there was not a building to be pointed to or named, nothing man-made; nothing.

The ships of the First Fleet were finally at rest, after eight months at sea, in what would be called Sydney Cove. Bewildered people looked out at an immensity of sky and light, at sun and sand and sea, rocks and trees. It was a frightening place, old and empty and utterly alien. Few of the 729 convicts (estimates vary) had heard of it until they found themselves gaoled and sentenced to transportation there for seven, for fourteen years, for life. For most there would be no return. This place was where they would spend the rest of their lives.

Disembarkation of the men began and sounds of axe and hammer split the great silence. From the ships, the women watched for another week while tents and huts grew where trees had been and the small settlement began to take shape. When it was time for them to go ashore they wore their best: bedraggled finery for some; for others, fair and cherished replicas of London fashion; for the rest, new 'slops' from store.

In a frenzied celebration of freedom and the feel of earth underfoot, men and women rushed together. One observer said, 'It is beyond my abilities to give a just description of the Scene of Debauchery and Riot that ensued during the night'.[1] Thunder, lightning and torrential rain put an end to the roistering.

Next morning Governor Arthur Phillip, who was in command of this extraordinary odyssey, called a general muster and dampened spirits were not uplifted during his castigation. He harangued. He threatened: All those practising 'promiscuous intercourse' and all men found in the women's camp after dark would be severely punished. Marriage, it seemed to the Governor, could be a solution to loose conduct.[2]

The Reverend Richard Johnson, Chaplain, agreed. Captain Watkin Tench, a shrewd observer, also thought marriage 'a good way to palliate the old habits of depravity'.[3] On the next Sunday, 10 February 1788, Reverend Johnson officiated at a mass marriage ceremony beneath the shade of a gum tree on the edge of the sand.

The women of the First Fleet were recorded then and have been lumped together ever since as a rampageous lot, as prostitutes, as 'damned whores'[4], as 'never a more abandoned set of wretches collected in any one place at any one time'.[5] It was undoubtedly true of many of them, though the new country and the new lifestyle and climate would bring changes.

Most of the 191 women (again estimates vary slightly) who arrived in the ships *Lady Penrhyn, Friendship, Charlotte* and *Prince of Wales* were rough and they were tough, necessary qualities for survival in late 18th-century England where life could be fine for the rich, execrable for the poor. It was the roughness and toughness of the women which carried them through the rigours of the gaols, the transports, the treatment which reflected the general attitude towards them of 'Chattels; Officers and Men for the Use of'. (This attitude did not prevent some lasting relationships, however. Officers and gentlemen lived with convict women and had children by them, sometimes acknowledged, sometimes not. Some famous colonial families began so.)

In Australia's early history women are elusive creatures who must be delved for. Were they deliberately written out? Omitted by official design? Or were they not considered as important enough to be recorded as anything other than statistics? This last seems likely, in step with the prevailing attitude towards women.

More resilient, more adaptable than the men, it was these women who produced the first Australian-born white children; survivors, like their mothers. It was these women who helped to turn bush huts into homes, worked on the land with the men, began to change a raw colony into a country to live in.

In England (where it was estimated that in London alone 110 000 people lived on the proceeds of crime), petty theft and prostitution had helped to supplement food and clothing for the women, but had also brought them into the dock at the Old Bailey or the provincial assizes, and into the crowded gaols. Prostitution alone was not grounds for transportation, but it seemed that at least one in five of the First Fleet women had been 'on the town'.

Common crimes among women were larceny, theft of clothing, theft of animals, robbery and receiving, wilful destruction, and vagrancy.[6] There were large numbers of servants and there were milliners, barmaids, dairymaids, needlewomen, a capmaker, stay-makers, mantua-makers (skilled dressmakers), a silk-weaver, a boot-closer, a pottery girl, one who said she was 'good for nothing', another who admitted to having been on the town but denied that she had ever picked pockets 'as the other girls did'.

The majority were in their twenties, though some were very young and a few were very old. Elizabeth Howard, clogmaker (seven years for stealing), was only thirteen. Dorothy Handlyn, alias Grey (seven years for stealing), was eighty-two! Elizabeth Beckford (72) was transported for shoplifting, Mary Love (60) for lamb-stealing.

There were many Ann(e)s. Ann Inett, a mantua-maker from Frimley in Worcestershire, was convicted in 1785 for stealing 'one dimity petticoat, three muslin handkerchiefs, one pair stuff shoes, one silk hood, one linen gown, one pair cotton stockings and one muslin cap, the goods and chattels of Jane Brookes, spinster'. Her sentence was hanging, commuted to transportation for seven years. Ann Inett was one of the six convict women chosen soon after the First Fleet's arrival to go as the first settlement group to Norfolk Island. She became the mistress of Philip Gidley King, the officer in charge. She bore him two sons, Sydney and Norfolk, in their first two years on the island. (In 1792 she married, in Sydney, a fellow convict who was later granted an absolute pardon by King, who was by then Governor of the colony.)

Elizabeths were also many. One of them, Elizabeth Lee (a cook), had committed a most dramatic offence. In 1785 she had been convicted of stealing '30 gallons of port, 12 gallons of Malmsey wine, 3 gallons of Madeira, claret, raisin wine, orange wine, brandy, rum, gin and arak, together with 424 glass bottles and 1 cwt of tallow candles, as well as 3 linen stocks, 2 pr stockings, 1 gold ring set with garnets and 2 crown pieces' from her employer!

The Marys were many; there were Sarahs, Margarets, Susans or Susannahs, a couple of Charlottes, a Rachel and an Isabella, two Esthers and some Kates, an Eleanor, a few Marthas, a Deborah, a Phebe, a Rebecca and a Hannah.

A Susannah and a Mary were two of the brides at that first mass wedding. Each had a young child and it was presumed in each case that the bridegroom was the father. This was certainly true of Henry Kable, united in matrimony that day to Susannah Holmes.[7]

In March 1774 Susannah Holmes, aged 19, had been sentenced to death for the theft of household linen and silver, the sentence commuted to seven years' transportation. In Norwich Gaol she met 19-year-old Henry Kable (Cabell) from Mendham in Suffolk, who had kept watch while his father and Abraham Carman robbed a country house. His death sentence had also been commuted, but he had had to watch the public hanging of his father and Carman on the green outside the gaol.

Susannah and Henry became lovers and in the spring of 1776 she gave birth to 'a fine boy', named Henry after his father; a devoted father, who repeatedly sought permission to marry but was refused.

The First Fleet was being made ready, and in October that year when her baby ('a very fine babe which the mother had suckled from birth') was five months old, Susannah was one of three women that the Norwich gaoler was ordered to escort to Plymouth to join the ships. Kable's requests to be allowed to marry her and to travel on the same ship were refused.

In the miserable November weather, under the care of the turnkey John Simpson, the women made the coach trip to Plymouth, travelling outside, and then waited three hours in an open boat to be taken aboard the ship. As Susannah handed up her baby she was ordered to give him back to the turnkey. The child was not on the captain's list! The frantic Susannah had to be forcibly taken on board. Had John Simpson not been a humane man, mother and child might not have come together again.

Determined to see justice done, Simpson took the child to London, left him with a reliable woman and went to the home of the Colonial Secretary, Lord Sydney, to put the case. He first saw a secretary, persuaded him to write an order to restore child to mother, and waited with it in the hall. When Lord Sydney appeared he told his tale again and Lord Sydney, vowing himself 'much affected', signed the order. A message was sent to Plymouth and an order also made that Kable should travel with his Susannah, having been married before sailing. Triumphant, Simpson returned to Norwich to bring Henry Kable the news. The marriage did not take place then, but Kable did travel on the *Friendship*, with Susannah and the baby, when she sailed with the First Fleet on 15 May 1787.

Turnkey Simpson had told his story widely while in London and sympathisers had subscribed £20 to buy a package of goods for the couple. It was pilfered during the voyage and later Henry brought an action against the captain in Sydney's first civil court of law. He was awarded £15 compensation, a handsome sum for the couple, by then well married.

The Norwich Gaol baby was the first of Susannah and Henry's eleven children. The family prospered. Henry, partner in the boatbuilding firm of Kable and Underwood, had many other business activities, some of them later taken over by his eldest son. Susannah, respected and respectable matriarch, died in November 1825 and was survived for another twenty-one years by her Henry, who died aged eighty-four.

Mary and William Bryant[8], though their astonishing escape story is better known, were not to enjoy any of the Kables' success or to share a stable and lasting relationship. Mary Broad, an illiterate 21-year-old servant from Cornwall, was sentenced at the Exeter Assizes for stealing, the death sentence changed to transportation. William Bryant, an experienced boatman and fisherman, was convicted for giving assistance to smugglers.

They were prisoners on the transport *Charlotte*, having earlier been incarcerated together in the prison hulk *Dunkirk*, one of the old warships no longer fit for active service and used as temporary gaols. There was, therefore, every chance that Bryant was the father of the baby described in the log of Surgeon John White: 'on the evening of the 8th of September, between the hours of 3 and 4, Mary Broad, a convict, was delivered of a fine girl'. Bryant became the legal father at the mass wedding ceremony.

Bryant, one of the few men with a real knowledge of fishing, was put in charge of the government fishing boat to help feed the hungry settlement. He and Mary had their own hut and he was officially recognised as a useful man. In the first two lean years the Bryants probably lived better than most. At one time they were deprived of their hut for a while because Bryant had been doing a little private trading, but the privilege was later restored. Mary had a son, Emanuel. She was a strong and shrewd helpmate to Bryant, who was making escape plans. His intentions were suspected and he was watched, but the need for constant coming and going between shore and harbour gave him freedom of movement. In a hole dug under the floor of their hut, the Bryants hid supplies for their planned journey. From a Dutch ship's captain in harbour William acquired a compass, quadrant, chart, musket, bedding and some food. He kept the six-oared government cutter in excellent order and had gathered seven other convicts as crew, some with knowledge of boats. At 11 p.m. on 28 March 1790 the Bryants (the children aged 3 and 1), Samuel Bird, William Morton, James Cox, James Martin, John Butcher, William Allen and Nathaniel Lilley set out for Koepang in Timor, a distance of 5236 kilometres.

It was an amazing, hazardous, storm-beset journey, with danger from natives when they landed along the coast and with many mishaps to the boat. Mary and the children bore their sufferings 'with fortitude', it was recorded. In sixty-one days they reached Timor, after a journey which would often be compared with that of Bligh of the *Bounty*. Their escape had been discovered at midnight, but they had a good start and pursuit was abandoned; it may not have been made with great determination, for the Bryants' bravery, daring and accomplishment were generally admired.

The tale they told in Timor of being survivors of a shipwreck was at first believed, and they were well treated. When the truth was discovered they were gaoled and were later given into the charge of Captain Edwards, RN, who was escorting the *Bounty* survivors back to England. A disciplinarian, he had no admiration for their astonishing feat and made the journey difficult for them. Early on the voyage back, in Batavia, the baby Emanuel died and, twenty-one days later, Will Bryant. Two other men died before they reached the Cape of Good

Hope. There they were transferred to HMS *Gorgon*, taking marines of the First Fleet back to England. Three-year-old Charlotte was the next to die, and was buried at sea. Mary Bryant, widow, aged 25, arrived in England alone, friendless, her adventures become nothing.

She was subject to British justice again and in July 1792 she heard a court pronounce that she be sent to Newgate to complete her original sentence. Mary's extraordinary story aroused public sympathy, however, and James Boswell was one who took a particular interest in her case. When she had completed her sentence and been given an unconditional pardon on 2 May 1793, Boswell arranged for her to return to her family in Cornwall. He also sent her a regular living allowance for some time.

Mary's story has been told and retold in differing versions, some of them romantic, none official. There is, however, a memento of that long voyage, in the Mitchell Library in Sydney. There is no scent left except the dry scent of history in a small packet of crumbled leaves of false sarsaparilla, which was used in early Sydney to make 'sweet tea'. Found among Boswell's relics in 1937, it is labelled 'leaves from Botany Bay, used as tea'. It had been a present from Mary Bryant.

Esther Abrahams

ESTHER AND JANE

In the crowd watching that multiple-marriage ceremony on a beach in summer 1788 were two women who would leave a a deeper mark on history than a convict thumbprint.

Esther Abrahams[1], sixth or seventh on most First Fleet lists, would have to wait twenty-six years for her marriage, colonial style. Long before it happened she had been, briefly, unofficial First Lady; unofficial because she was still only the mistress of George Johnston, though she had lived with him from the earliest days. Johnston's name stands out again and again in Australia's early history. Esther's name has to be excavated from journals, letters and official records. Johnston looked what he was, an officer and a gentleman, well-built, of excellent family; a fair, handsome man, already distinguished in battle, who became a public hero after he 'put down' the Castle Hill convict rebellion in 1804. When Johnston arrested Governor Bligh on 27 January 1808 he issued a proclamation of peace and signed it himself as Lieutenant-Governor, thereby briefly making Esther, acknowledged mistress of his home, de facto First Lady. It was an extraordinary peak of fortune to be reached by a destitute Jewish convict girl.

In London in 1786 Esther Abrahams, milliner, a dark-eyed girl aged about 17, found herself pregnant, abandoned and desperate. She stole some black Spanish lace from a shop and was quickly followed and accused. She denied the charge, but when shaken, the lace fell from beneath her shawl and she was arrested. She was convicted on 7 August and sent to Newgate Prison. There she gave birth to a daughter, Rosanna, in March 1787. Two months later Esther and the baby sailed on the *Lady Penrhyn* with the First Fleet: eleven small ships setting off for the far side of the world to found a colony with its convicts, its marines, its officials.

On board also was Lieutenant George Johnston.[2] He was the son of Captain George Johnston of Annandale, Scotland, aide-de-camp to Lord Percy, later Duke of Northumberland. This connection would prove useful to the younger George, who had served England during the American War of Independence. In 1771 he had been wounded in action against the French in the East Indies. He sailed with the First Fleet as a First Lieutenant of the marine detachment that would garrison the new settlement. He was also, for a time, ADC to Governor Hunter.

Unlike many gentlemen who lived with convict women, Johnston acknowledged his de facto wife Esther, and always acknowledged and protected his children. Their first son was baptised on 4 March 1790 as George, son of George Johnston, Captain-Lieutenant of Marines, and of Esther Abrahams. At the christening of their second son Robert three years later,

Governor Phillip stood as godfather. Robert became the first Australian-born officer in the Royal Navy. The third son, David, became a grazier and there were four daughters, Maria, Julia, Isabella (died aged 2) and Blanche, who lived on until the early years of the twentieth century—a long, strong link with the colony's beginning.

Johnston's first land grant of 100 acres (40·5 hectares) was called Annandale, after his Scottish birthplace. The property grew to 1053 hectares and the large house expanded to become a mansion, a showplace reached by an avenue of Norfolk pines brought back as seedlings from a year of military duty on Norfolk Island. It was surrounded by what was almost a self-contained village: orchards, gardens, pastures, bakery, blacksmith, butchery, stores. Esther managed it most competently while Johnston was away in England awaiting trial in 1800, and court-martial for mutiny in 1811 following the Bligh arrest. He was fortunate both times, his army record and his influential patron, the Duke of Northumberland, being strongly effective. The trial was quashed; as a result of the court-martial he was cashiered from the army but allowed to return to Sydney as a private citizen, arriving back at the end of May 1813.

For Esther they had been anxious years. With Johnston away her position was weakened, and if he did not return—a court-martial could have meant hanging—that position and her property would be at risk. She was a strong-minded and passionate woman, quick-tempered and necessarily firm with her servants. At Annandale she was mistress of sixteen former convicts and her own ascent up the social ladder from a similar background could bring taunts and accusations if she did not rule carefully.

Annandale was such a fine and prosperous property that many land-hungry gentlemen in Sydney would have been delighted to grab this attractive piece of real estate from 'Johnston's woman, a Jew'. During this time she began to call herself Mrs Julian, which conferred a more solid respectability (it may also have been the name of Rosanna's father).

As Mrs Esther Julian she applied for a land grant and was given one in the Georges River district. It was later revoked by Governor Macquarie, a man of high moral principles who would have known her background well and who thoroughly—and publicly, in the pages of the *Sydney Gazette*—deplored 'the pernicious custom of people of the opposite sex living together and cohabiting without the sanctity of matrimony'. Esther held on to the land and eventually a fine house, George's Hall, was built there on the river bank. It became the home of the grazier son, David, and Esther's home during her last years.

After his return Johnston became a favourite of Governor Macquarie and it was probably at the Governor's strong instigation that Esther and George were married on 12 November 1814. (As he was no longer an army officer, Johnston was also by then free to make his own choice of wife.) Their eldest son, George, was twenty-five. Witnesses to the certificate of marriage were Rosanna and Isaac Nicholls, Esther's first child and her husband, former convict become convict overseer, hotel licensee, landowner and postmaster.

Macquarie took an interest in the Johnston children. He appointed George, the eldest son, a clerk to the Commissary and later Deputy Provost Marshal. George was an excellent horseman and had earned fame by successfully rounding up the valuable herd of wild cattle which had bred from the seven that had strayed in 1788. He was killed in a riding accident during a cattle muster in February 1820. His grieving mother found solace in the Governor's commissioning of a marble mausoleum, to be designed by Francis Greenway and built on the family property.

Three years later, Esther's husband was laid to rest in the same vault.

Now there were more difficult days. Johnston had left the Annandale estate 'to the mother of my children for the term of her natural life' and to Robert on her death. Robert very much resented his mother's management and there were many quarrels. She continued to manage Annandale, but in 1829 told the family she was going to mortgage it so she could return to England.

Robert took drastic steps. He brought a court action to have his mother declared unfit to manage the property—in fact, to have her declared insane. Esther, known to have a hot temper and a fondness for strong drink, lost the case, though she was not judged totally insane. (It was generally agreed among court officials that if all those in Sydney town known to enjoy drink were to be declared insane, few would be left to look after the township.) Robert was not judged 'heir at law', however, and trustees were appointed.

Esther left Annandale to live with David at George's Hall, the property which had been her own land grant. She died there in August 1846 and was buried with her husband in the splendid Greenway mausoleum in the garden at Annandale. As in life, there was a subsidiary role for Esther . . .

> Sacred to the Memory of George Johnston of Annandale, *formerly of HM 102nd Regiment with which he arrived in this colony 26 January 1788. Died 5 January 1823, aged 58 years. Also Esther relict of the above d. 26 August 1846, aged 75.*

In 1878 the vault was moved to Waverley Cemetery, where it is still. Within, too, lie Isabella, the daughter who died at 2; sons George, David and Robert—Commander Johnston, RN, who died in 1882 aged 92; his wife Selina and some of their seven sons; and many, many Johnston descendants.

Johnston Street, Annandale, is a permanent reminder of the family. Robert lived in the house until his own death. The property had been subdivided and the house was demolished in about 1904, after 105 years of family occupation.

Despite her brief spell as unofficial First Lady, Esther never lived at Government House; but Jane Dundas[3] did. Almost her whole life in the colony was spent in service there, first with Governor Phillip, then with Grose, Paterson and King. This tenuous Government House link is the only apparent connection between Esther and Jane. They both arrived as convicts with the First Fleet—albeit on different ships—but in the gossipy, rampageous, argumentative little settlement each would certainly have known the other's name. Sydney was a very small town.

To Jane, one of the convict women on board the *Prince of*

Wales, the honour of a state funeral in the distant future would have seemed ludicrous. She was a quiet country girl, one of many such girls tempted to leave rural life for the pleasures and good fortune of London. She worked there as a laundry maid in the household of Sir John Skinner and (according to the Skinner butler, who gave a character reference at her trial) she had been an excellent maid who 'behaved vastly well always, bore a good character, a quiet sober girl'.

Jane's downfall was the passion in England for lotteries which offered big prizes. The 'quiet sober girl' had no money for tickets, so stole some linen to pawn in order to get some. She was caught, tried at the Old Bailey in 1773 for stealing and sentenced to seven years' transportation. She confessed she had 'stolen for the lottery' but intended to redeem the linen later.

Good conduct and quiet demeanour brought rewards. By 1790 Jane was housemaid to Governor Phillip and later became his housekeeper, 'my good Dundas'. Her life from then on was passed in government service, though she could have chosen otherwise. When Philip Gidley King and his new wife Anna Josepha, expecting their first child, went to Norfolk Island, the reliable Jane went with them. She had found her niche in life. In the Kings' first official 'residence' on Norfolk (a tiny, primitive stone cottage) Jane assisted at the birth of their only son, the future Admiral Phillip Parker King.

When the Kings went back to England, Jane went with them. She had completed her sentence on Norfolk and could certainly have remained in England, a free woman with excellent references. Instead she returned to New South Wales with them on the ship *Speedy* in 1799. King was coming out as the new Governor.

It was not an easy voyage. There was a good deal of illness among the convict women, and the ship's doctor was not only physically ill, but became mentally unstable. In Cape Town he was pronounced insane, and his head shaved and blistered. Mrs King wrote later: 'his health seems better but extremely weak and *to me he looks mad and acts mad*'. During rough weather Jane Dundas had a bad fall. Mrs King:

Dundas has just fallen down the companion stairs and has dreadfully bruised her back, ribs and one foot. She can scarcely move nor can she lie in bed, every time the ship gives a lurch she is ready to scream out with pain.[4]

Back in Sydney, Jane became the Kings' much-valued housekeeper. She was given the courtesy title of Mrs Dundas and was known (and, it seems, admired) by many of the Government House visitors. She was also known as Jeanette, instead of the plainer Jane. That Jane was accorded respect and affection by many within the Government House circle was evidenced by messages received after her death in December 1805, when she was 57 years old. The Governor, his wife, some of their friends and officials attended the funeral service, having first joined in a private tribute at Government House. On the memorial stone over her grave the Governor had these words inscribed: 'an honest, faithful and affectionate servant, which character the deceased maintained during a service of fifteen years'.

During those years Jane had received numerous little presents and tributes from her employers and their friends. She had nursed many visiting officials when they became ill, and their grateful gifts had been tucked away with her treasures. Jane had become a jackdaw, the sober personality coloured and satisfied by contemplation of her possessions. Her personal effects, listed for sale in the *Gazette* some time later, made an intriguing and curious array. The advertisement read:

To be sold by auction by Mr David Beavan in his rooms in South Street on Wednesday next the 2nd of April in the afternoon. The following Wearing Apparel and other Property of the late Mrs J. Dundas deceased.

The long, double-column list included:

. . . 1 White Muslin Gown, 2 coloured ditto, 1 silk ditto, 10 cotton ditto, 3 dimity petticoats, 1 muslin ditto, 13 ditto of various kinds, 1 straw and coloured bonnet, 14 pairs of shoes, 2 half Norwich shawls, 1 muslin ditto, 8 coloured ditto, 24 pocket handkerchiefs, 8 silk ditto, 7 coloured ditto, 22 muslin neck ditto, 8 half ditto, 1 muslin apron, 12 coloured ditto, 6 Irish and 10 calico shifts, 10 habit shirts, 2 muslin ditto, 2 muslin frills, 1 muslin bonnet, 1 cloak, 1 black veil,

1 pair of silk gloves, 1 pair of nankeen ditto, 3 pairs of nankeen stays, 1 muslin cap, 1 flannel bedgown, 1 brush and comb, a pair of drawers, 24 pairs of plain hose, 3 pairs worsted ditto, 6 pairs of clock hose, 1 pair of silk ditto, 1 blue cloth great coat, 12 double bordered and 1 plain cap . . .

It is an impressive catalogue. Shoes and stockings were very expensive. How would Jane have acquired twenty-four pairs of plain hose, plus the worsted, the silk and the clock hose? Many yards of various materials were listed; lengths of lace and threads and trimmings, sufficient needles to stock a haberdashery counter; and personal belongings such as a quantity of old books, two watches, one large chest, one writing desk and five pencils, and a small cabin trunk.

Wrapped in these layers of possessions—hidden in shawls and habit shirts, 63 yards of tape, 112 'skanes' of thread, twenty-two muslin neckerchiefs, five pairs of dimity and duck pockets *and* 6¼ yards buglabore (no dictionary definition as yet for this)—is the girl Jane, Sir John Skinner's laundrymaid ('behaved vastly well always'), the woman Mrs Jeanette Dundas ('an honest, faithful and affectionate servant'), confidante and friend to Anna Josepha King, nurse to her children and to lonely, hard-drinking, ailing military gentlemen who fell ill while guests at Government House.

Elizabeth Macarthur

THE CAPTAIN'S WIFE — ELIZABETH MACARTHUR

Towards the end of June 1790 the ships of the Second Fleet had begun to arrive in Sydney. By then it had become a desperate little town. No ships had come for so long; its people were hungry, their clothes torn and ragged, feet often bare, hearts starting to despair that the rest of the world had forgotten them.

Welcome though the ships were, they could have been more happily provisioned. There *was* food, but there was also a new supply of women convicts, 221 of them aboard the *Lady Juliana*. According to Marine John Nicol, whose journal on the voyage was published some thirty years later, the women were a lively lot, among them 'Mrs Barnsley, a noted card-sharper and shoplifter who openly boasted that her family had been swindlers and highwaymen for the last two hundred years'.[1] She was always very kind to the other women, he said, generous and helpful, acting as midwife when needed. She was 'a queen amongst them all'.

Sarah Whitelam was one of the girls in need of her services and it was Marine Nicol himself who was the father of her child. He wrote:

> *Once we put to sea every man on board took a wife from among the convicts, they nothing loath. I must confess I was as bad on this point as the others. The girl with whom I lived was Sarah Whitelam, a native of Lincoln, a girl of modest and reserved turn, as kind and true a creature as ever lived. I courted her for a week and upward and would have wed her on the spot if there had been a clergyman on board. I fixed my fancy upon her from the moment I* knocked the rivets out of her irons.[2]

Sarah and her son remained alone in Sydney. Nicol had asked permission to marry her, but was refused. He sailed for England, vowing to return as soon as possible. Like so many convict girls, Sarah was left to get on with life and bring up her boy as best she could.

Like Sarah—and Esther and Jane, Susannah and Mary—the women of the First Fleet and Second Fleet were not all hardened criminals. Some claimed to be *ladies!* Augusta Hipsley said she was a daughter of a colonel in the Royal Dragoons. Her three brothers were all naval or army officers. She herself was competent to teach drawing, music, singing, French and fancy needlework. She was transported for pawning a shawl she did not own and had a previous conviction for forgery. Marine Nicol's journal also mentioned 'a pretty well-behaved girl rumoured to be the illegitimate daughter of a British Prime Minister' and 'a young cultured Scots girl who kept herself to herself and cried a great deal; died of a broken heart before the ship sailed'.

There *was* a lady with the Second Fleet, the undoubted

genuine English article, a gently bred country girl from a respectable, well-established farming background—Elizabeth Macarthur, the Captain's wife. She brought gentility and the graces of good feminine company to the limited little social circle around Government House. Because of her, Australian history, otherwise sparse in memorable sayings, has its own nine-word phrase to echo through 200 years: 'There will always be a roll for Mrs Macarthur'. Gentlemen dining at Government House were asked to bring their own bread, for even Government House was on rations and Phillip had sent his private foodstock, flour included, to the Public Store. But there was bread for Elizabeth. If Mrs Barnsley had been queen on board the *Lady Juliana*, Elizabeth Macarthur deserved to be called 'the queen of Sydney town'.

Elizabeth's first impressions had not been good:

> ... *save for the natural setting of the finest harbour in the known world everything was wretched, the filthy ships in the Cove, the rude lines of sodden barracks, the tents that held the sick sagging in the downpour along the waterfront; the night fires in the region of the Rocks, a sink of evil already and more like a gipsy encampment than part of a town.*[3]

She wrote well, with a nice feeling for the subtleties of language, though she could also be long-winded, in the mode of the day. On the voyage out John Macarthur had been very ill with rheumatic fever.

> *It continued to rage till every sense was lost and every faculty but life destroyed. My little boy was at that time so very ill that I could scarcely expect him to survive a day. Alone, unfriended and in such a situation what do I not owe to a merciful God for granting me support and assistance in these severe moments of affliction.*

Elizabeth did many things well but remained modest, a perfect wife and companion for the difficult, argumentative and aggressive man in whose enormous shadow she would walk. She loved him deeply always and was that rare creature, a truly happy human being. 'I can truly say no two people on earth can be happier than we are' she wrote years later to her old friend Bridget Kingdon in England.

> . . . *in Mr Macarthur's society I experience the tenderest affection of a husband. He is instructive and cheerful as a companion, an indulgent father, beloved as a master and universally respected for the integrity of his character. Judge then, my friend, if I ought not to consider myself a happy woman.*

It was a view of John Macarthur that few people in Sydney town would have shared.

Elizabeth Veale[4] was the daughter of Richard Veale, a yeoman farmer with 38 hectares in the Tamar Valley in Devonshire. Her father died quite young and her mother remarried. The young Elizabeth spent much time in the vicarage in the neighbouring village of Bridgerule, home of the Reverend John Kingdon, MA, a former Fellow of Exeter College, Cambridge. She was almost as much a part of the family as was her close friend Bridget, his eldest daughter. She did lessons with the family and wrote letters to them during all her long life in Australia. It may have been in their house that she met a young military officer named John Macarthur.

The son of a linen draper in Plymouth, he had been in the army since he was 15 or 16, an ensign then with the Corps of Foot. After the American War of Independence, like many young officers he was put on half-pay. He studied both law and farming before rejoining a regiment, the 68th Foot. John Macarthur and Miss Elizabeth Veale had been godparents at the christening in May 1788 of the Kingdons' youngest daughter. They were married by the Reverend Kingdon in October 1788.

Edward, the first Macarthur child, was born in 1789. In June that year John was appointed a lieutenant in the New South Wales Corps, which was being formed for service in the new colony. Both the Macarthurs saw this venture as a chance of financial advancement and Elizabeth looked forward to their new life. Her main regret was that she would be separated from her mother, but the journey itself did not dismay her. Not quite 21, she had previously seen herself as being timid and irresolute and was pleased with this new feeling of strength and adventure.

On 13 November 1789 the Macarthurs and baby Edward embarked on the *Neptune*, which carried seventy-eight female convicts, 421 male convicts and two officers of the New South Wales Corps, Captain Nepean and Lieutenant Macarthur. It was not long before John Macarthur and the ship's captain, John Gilbert, were engaged in fierce arguments and at Plymouth they fought a duel. They agreed to try to live peacefully together, but Captain Gilbert was such a difficult man that the authorities replaced him. Elizabeth's rejoicings in this were replaced by doubts very soon, 'for the disagreeable truth', she wrote in her journal, 'is that Mr Traill's character was of a much blacker hue'.

The weather was bad, and so many things went wrong with the ship that they did not set sail until late December.

The Macarthurs were to share a big upper cabin with Captain Nepean, who gave permission for his space to be partitioned off for women convicts. This made the Macarthurs' half completely dark, and the common passage used by them and by what Elizabeth termed 'the abandoned creatures next door' caused her great distress, being always filled with convicts 'and their constant attendants, filth and vermin'. There were so many arguments between Macarthur, his senior officer, Nepean, and the ship's captain that application was made for transfer to another ship, and on a day when the weather was right for it the Macarthurs transferred to the *Scarborough*. They found conditions much better; life became happier.

Later the baby became very sick and in Cape Town, while helping to get some drunken soldiers back on board, Macarthur was drenched with sea water and developed rheumatic fever, from which he recovered very slowly. The baby's health improved, but the months at sea, the strains and trials and real physical fear felt during storms had toughened Elizabeth's gentle spirit and character — good training for the future, when she would be completely in charge of a large family, a home and a very large property, directing all to a state of prosperity during the eleven years her husband would spend in England.

She was a capable woman, generous and lively, compassionate and helpful, yet with one strange lack. She seemed never to feel any kind of sympathy for the convict women, not a tinge of emotion nor a thought for the kind of experiences that had sent them to the colony. Her own feelings are fully described in her letters, theirs never even imagined. The gap between *them* and *us* was absolute.

The first two years, though lonely, were enjoyable and she found the climate delightful: 'I have never known such bright warm winter weather'. Macarthur had been the first officer to bring his *lady* wife with him and Elizabeth very much missed the company of women friends, though she enjoyed the engagements at Government House and the special place she occupied at the dinner table there, with Governor Arthur Phillip and his officers making much of her.

After the arrival of the *Gorgon* in September 1791, life became much livelier. Anna Josepha King came, accompanying her husband to Norfolk Island, as did Mrs Parker, wife of the *Gorgon*'s captain. Elizabeth found them both good company.

> . . . *we have spent many pleasant days together. One of the agents of Transports has also his wife with him so that our little circle is of late quite brilliant. We are constantly making little parties in boats up and down the various inlets of the Harbour, taking refreshments with us and dining out under an awning upon some pleasant point of land.*

A daughter Elizabeth was born to the Macarthurs and then came James, who died at 11 months and was later replaced by another James. (It was a usual practice, in a time of high infant mortality, to give the same name to another baby.) The Macarthurs moved to Parramatta, then named Rose Hill, in June 1791. John had become Regimental Paymaster, with a better salary, but was itching to get some land and begin to expand his life.

The first land grant was in February 1793, 100 acres (40·5 hectares) at Parramatta. The next year a further 100 acres were awarded as a prize for the first officer to get 50 acres under cultivation. Elizabeth was given a cow and a calf: 'To a family in this country in its present situation it is a gift beyond value.'

The house they built (and which still stands at Parramatta) was named, after her, Elizabeth Farm.[6] It was a brick building 68 feet long and 18 feet wide (20·7 m x 5·5 m), with a kitchen and servants' quarters behind. The farm extended for 101·25 hectares, much of it cleared and more than 40 hectares under cultivation by August 1794 when Elizabeth described it in a letter to her mother. They sold £400 of produce that year and had 1800 bushels (65·5 m³) of corn in store, 20 acres (8·1 hectares) under wheat and 80 acres (32·4 hectares) being readied for potatoes and more corn. In the letter she advised of:

> ... having been brought to bed of a very fine Boy, to whom I have given his father's name, John. He, with Edward and Elizabeth are in perfect health and promise fairly to become everything we could desire.

A year later she had said goodbye to Edward, sent to England for his education, a practice strongly believed by most socially secure people in the colony to ensure a better future for the children. 'My dear Edward almost quitted me without a tear', Elizabeth wrote. Her own tears she sternly suppressed, as she did later when she had to say goodbye to Elizabeth and John. They went to England in 1800 with Macarthur, who had been granted leave to pursue his affairs there. John was then 7 and his mother was never to see him again. He died in London at the age of 30, a promising lawyer, always busy on his family's business and a regular correspondent with his beloved mother.

Young Elizabeth, whose health was too delicate for the English climate, came back to Parramatta with her father the next year. With them came Miss Penelope Lucas, who was to be the Macarthurs' governess and Elizabeth Macarthur's devoted friend and confidante for the next thirty years. Elizabeth had then, at last, an intelligent woman of her own class and education with whom she could share hopes, fears, gossip, elation, domestic worries and triumphs. With them also came John's nephew, Hannibal Hawkins Macarthur, who would eventually marry Maria King, daughter of Governor Philip Gidley King and Anna Josepha.

After his return, while the senior officer (Lieut-Colonel Paterson) was away and Macarthur, was in temporary military command, he became involved in a fearsome dispute with Governor King. It led to a duel between Macarthur and Paterson, who was wounded in the shoulder. Macarthur was arrested and sent to England in 1801 for court-martial, although he avoided this. He was eventually allowed to resign his commission and returned to Sydney, a private citizen, in 1805.

During his frequent long absences, Elizabeth confidently and capably managed the farm, the family, the servants and workmen, and the increasing flock of sheep which had become her husband's particular interest. She missed John and kept him in touch with the affairs of Elizabeth Farm through frequent letters. Macarthur, a man who always *knew* that he was in the right and that his way was best, had complete confidence in his wife's abilities.

> *I am perfectly aware, my beloved wife, of the difficulties you have to contend with, and fully convinced that not one woman in a thousand (no one that I know) would have resolution and perseverance to contend with them all, much more to surmount them in the manner you have so happily done. That I am grateful and delighted with your conduct I think it is needless for me to say.*

It was during his absence that the 1804 Castle Hill rising took place. There was a night in which Elizabeth and her family were in danger; the farm was also under threat of fire. Elizabeth was in Parramatta having tea with Mrs Marsden, wife of the Reverend Samuel Marsden. Her youngest children, James and Mary, were with her and some women friends. It had seemed expedient for women and children to drive to Sydney for safety and they had left at 11 p.m., seeing the flames of burning buildings as they left. In writing of it to John, her choice of words was again admirable:

> *... we arrived in Sydney about 3 o'clock in the morning. The Town was all in arms. The Marines from the* Calcutta *disembarked and a great number of the sailors armed. Most of the officers were on shore and kindly received us, poor fugitives, at the wharf. We had determined to take up our abode at Mr Marsden's house ... to this house then* we and our little frightened sleepy tribe *were escorted.*

The affairs of the colony began to bound forward and the local affairs of the Macarthurs showed equal progress. While in England John had sought, and received, a magnificent land grant of 2025 hectares in the Cowpastures district (named for the herd of animals that had bred there from the original escapees of the earliest days). This property was called Camden Park and John planned to build a great house there. Meanwhile a new Governor was in Sydney: Bligh had replaced Philip Gidley King and from the beginning there was bad feeling between Governor and grazier. It culminated in the arrest of Macarthur and finally of George Johnston's march to Government House to depose Governor Bligh on 26 January 1808. Once again Macarthur was ordered to England, where he would be a witness at Johnston's court-martial. With him this time went the two youngest boys, James and William, leaving Elizabeth (still in delicate health), Mary and (soon) the youngest child, Emmeline, with their mother.

It was 1817 before Macarthur was allowed to return to the colony, but he and the older sons Edward (now in the British Army) and John were ever active in seeking advancement for their own and for the colony's business in England. John wrote to his wife: 'It will be the study of my life to requite you for all that you suffered on my account.'

It is doubtful whether she actually suffered a great deal, for she enjoyed her years of management—found them tremendously rewarding and satisfying. The Cowpastures property was well established; at Elizabeth Farm she built a new woolshed and in 1813 had 1300 ewes in lamb. She coped with troublesome natives, a drought, high prices, wheat crops burned. She studied the needs of the land, asked advice from experts and achieved several 'firsts'. She was the first farmer to make hay and to sell it and the first to pull out the tree-stumps when the land was cleared. In recognition of her achievements, Governor Macquarie granted her 243 hectares of land in her own name in the Parramatta district. She was always a welcome guest at Government House, and now there were bread rolls for everybody.

Emmeline, born when Elizabeth was 42, was her last child. The girls were educated at home and were trained, too, to be as industrious as their mother always was. They did all their own sewing: muslin dresses for summer, night attire, underwear, flannels for the men. They knew how to work in the dairy, to make fruit preserves, jam, candles. Breakfast was sometimes eaten as early as 5 a.m. Convicts were well treated, well fed and reasonably clothed. On Sunday they assembled for church (Catholics in one room, Protestants in another).

Her ill health did not prevent suitors asking for the hand of daughter Elizabeth. Surveyor-General John Oxley was one, William Charles Wentworth another; but she never married.

When Macarthur returned in 1817, with the sons James and William become young men, Elizabeth was enraptured to have so many of her family with her again. The boys settled at the Camden Park property and John Macarthur took back the reins of management that his wife had held so capably. Her letters now became more concerned with family and social affairs; then, after Macarthur's deterioration and his mental breakdown, lovingly concerned for him. He ordered his wife and daughters out of Elizabeth Farm and the girls stayed with Penelope Lucas at Hambleden, the delightful Georgian cottage that had been built for her. Elizabeth wrote:

> *I cannot say that the blow, severe as it is, has come upon us without long previous apprehension that sooner or later, that mighty mind would break down and give way.*

John finally went to stay at Camden Park, where James and William could look after him and where he could take an interest in the house being built, in the garden and horses. When the news of his death came to Elizabeth, staying in Sydney with her daughter Mary Bowman, whose fourth child had just been born, she wrote to her son Edward in England: 'I know you will weep, dearest Edward, and indeed the fountains of my eyes which I believed almost dry have been opened anew.'

That was in 1834. Elizabeth died in 1850, aged 83, still grieving deeply over the death of her eldest daughter six years earlier. Elizabeth was buried at Camden Park. She had never been back to England, though in her later years she thought wistfully of doing so. Through her letters to her sons and to her friend Miss Kingdon she reveals the life of the colony and her total involvement in it.

She could be shrewish: 'The Law Department is a complete

pest. When these people come here they represent themselves as Pillars of the Colony. I think they prove to be Caterpillars!'

Of her daughter Emmeline there is a neat little character study. It follows a description of a party at Government House at which Emmeline had played the piano, Miss Macdouggal the harp. 'Emmeline is a tall girl fond of butterflies and flowers.'

Of herself: 'I am a truly happy woman'.[5]

Anna Josepha

ANNA JOSEPHA — FIRST LADY

In the quiet, Jane Austen kind of world of Hatherleigh in Devonshire towards the end of 1790, the arrival of Lieutenant Philip Gidley King must have seemed a thrilling event to the district's young ladies. Into a place of simple pleasures and rural domesticity, of long visits to and from friends and relatives, country walks and gossip about neighbours, new fashions and embroidery stitches, arrived a man who might have come from outer space.

He was an emissary from the Governor of New South Wales, Captain Arthur Phillip, sent to report to the British Government on the parlous state of the new colony, its pressing needs for food, clothing, seeds, tools, farm animals and household goods. The stories he had to tell of his First Fleet voyage to that extraordinary land—talk of wild seas, rough convicts, hardships and achievements—blew like an invigorating sea breeze through country drawing rooms. Anna Josepha Coombe[1], aged 26, found the tales told by her first cousin, this much-travelled 33-year-old Cornishman, as irresistible as she found the man himself.

They were married at St Martin-in-the-Fields in London in March 1791, a hastily arranged marriage which neither would ever wish to repent at leisure. She was an admirable and loving wife for a man who would later be regarded often as testy and irritable, and he was always devoted to his Anna and to his family. Circumstances of the engagement are speculative only. A family story said that he met her at a ball the week before he was to depart, proposed immediately and was accepted. It is also possible that, with all the family visitings of the time, they had known each other since childhood and had formed an 'attachment'. However it happened, King had found for himself 'treasure upon earth'. She was an ideal wife for a man whose life would have many tribulations.

The wedding had to be arranged quickly, for King had been promoted to Commander, had been appointed Lieutenant-Governor of Norfolk Island and had received orders to sail as soon as possible. His bride would scarcely have had time to think seriously about the enormous changes about to take place in her life, to say her goodbyes and to pack her baggage before she was aboard HMS *Gorgon*, bound for Sydney, on a six-month voyage into the unknown.

King was an honourable man. He would no doubt have told her that the small, isolated Norfolk Island, which could have been a Pacific paradise, was instead a gaol, a convict settlement and at times a place of desperation. He would also have confessed news that would have sent many young ladies of the time into a fit of the vapours; that in his two years on Norfolk Island he had sired two sons by a convict woman. She accepted the news with equanimity, as she later accepted the two children into her own family.[2]

In 1788 Governor Phillip singled King out as a reliable and capable officer and gave him the unenviable task of establishing a second convict settlement on Norfolk Island. Even before women convicts had been landed from the First Fleet's *Lady Penrhyn*, King had been asked to go on board to consult with the surgeon, Lieutenant Bowes, about the characters of the women and choose five or six to go to Norfolk. In his journal Bowes wrote:

> He has made choice of such of both sexes whose behaviour on board during the voyage has been the least exceptionable and has held out such encouragement upon their behaving properly as must render their situation much more comfortable than it would have been at Port Jackson . . . he also informed them that it was the Governor's pleasure, that if any partiality or reciprocal affection shd. take place between the Male & Female Convicts going there or after their arrival at Norfolk they might marry & that he had authorized the Surgeon, Mr Jameson to perform that Office & after a time the Clergyman. wd. be sent there to remarry them.

For one of the six women chosen, Ann Inett, it was Lieutenant King who formed 'a partiality'. She lived with him on Norfolk and had two sons, Norfolk (the first white child to be born there) and Sydney. King always acknowledged and looked after the boys. Years later, as Governor, he granted Ann's husband, also a convict, an absolute pardon.

The voyage on the *Gorgon* was a reasonably good one, made particularly enjoyable for Anna Josepha by the company of Mrs Parker, wife of the captain, and a young man called William Chapman. (Only 17, he was being sponsored by Governor Phillip, would become a clerk on Norfolk Island and would be absolutely devoted to Mrs King.) Both were lively and constant letter-writers and left first-hand accounts of the voyage out: Mrs Parker's *Voyage Round the World in the Gorgon* and William Chapman's letters to his mother and sister.[3]

Mrs King was an admirable sailor who seems never to have been seasick, and she greatly enjoyed ten days of jolly hospitality and exploring at Tenerife. Here the Commander had a very bad fall from a staircase and injured an arm, which worried his wife deeply. Their next port was St Jago in the Cape Verde Islands, where they met the four transports they were escorting to New South Wales. Here Mrs King met a woman who was to become a close friend—Mrs Paterson, wife of Captain Paterson of the New South Wales Corps.

In Cape Town they stayed on shore, enjoying the hospitality of Mr Peter de Witt, a prosperous merchant, and his mother. Mrs Parker found the women of Cape Town 'remarkably large', and considered that this was because they went without stays and spent most of their time sitting with their feet continually lifted on a chair!

Though the coast of New South Wales was sighted on 11 September 1791, rough weather delayed their landing for a week. King, returning to a familiar place, was able to point out remembered features as he and his wife made their way to Government House to be the guests of Governor Phillip at a small dinner party that night to celebrate the *Gorgon*'s safe arrival.

There were many parties and picnics. Elizabeth Macarthur, for so long the sole feminine adornment of Government House dinners, had at last the company she had craved: 'Our little circle is of late quite brilliant', she wrote. 'Mrs King is possessed of a great share of good nature and frankness ... Mrs Parker is very amiable and intelligent.'

The good times soon finished, for the Kings were to leave for Norfolk Island on the *Atlantic*. Anna Josepha was delighted that Captain and Mrs Paterson would accompany them and that there was a surgeon on board, because she was pregnant and anxious to get settled as quickly as possible. They were given a grand send-off, accompanied to the end of Sydney Cove by the Governor, the Judge-Advocate and Captain and Mrs Parker.

Getting on and off Norfolk was notoriously dependent on the weather, and Mrs King was pleased that strong wind delayed their landing for only a day. The shabby little building (only 3·6 metres by 7·3 metres) which was to be her home could scarcely have raised her spirits, for every part of it seemed in disrepair, but she 'made do'. She even managed to accommodate William Chapman, who was to be the island's official storekeeper, and King's son Norfolk, who had journeyed from Sydney with them. Her own son, Phillip Parker King, was born there six weeks later.

On their first Sunday there was an official ceremony. The officers were asked to dinner—apparently in that small house, prisoners were pardoned for local crimes and the Reverend Richard Johnson, who had come from Sydney for this purpose, performed a welter of weddings and christenings.

In the seventeen months since King had left it, the relatively even tenor of island life had changed and he wrote to the Under-Secretary in London:

> I landed here on the 4th instant, when I found discord and strife on every person's countenance, and in every corner of the island. I am pestered with complaints, bitter revilings and almost everything to begin over again.

King could not achieve the peaceful and merciful rule he had desired. He suffered from gout and his health was poor. He could not have been an easy husband, but in the first fifteen months at least Anna Josepha was very happy, for she had her friend Mrs Paterson for company. After the Patersons left, there were no other officers' wives until it was almost time for the Kings, too, to depart.

Two more Kings were born on the island: Maria in 1793 and in 1795 a delicate little girl called Utricia (a family name), who died several years later. Anna was sometimes ill and her husband suffered from violent attacks of gout. For medical assistance there was a convict 'bred to surgery' and Darcy Wentworth, who had some medical training and had come out with the Second Fleet as a free settler (he was fortunate not to have come as a convict, given his dubious record of assaults and robbery). By 1795 King's health was so bad that his life was despaired of and he asked William Chapman to take charge of his papers and his family and to see that both were taken to England. He recovered, but was very worried about the future. His salary was only £250 per year, plus his half-pay as a naval commander, and there was no private income. He was scornful of officers who made themselves rich in the colony, and wrote: 'as I have neither kept a shop or sold drams, my wordly savings do not exceed £1000. I shall not return a Nabob.'

They arrived back in England in May 1797 after a long and arduous trip during which Anna's third daughter, Elizabeth, was born. Back home, King continued to brood about his future. Governor Phillip had recommended King as his successor, but Hunter had been appointed instead. Eventually King was told that he would take over from Hunter, but it was months before a ship was ready, the first one having been condemned. Money was very low by the time they sailed on the *Speedy* in November 1799. As King had received a little financial help because of delays, they were able to afford to leave Phillip Parker King at Naval School in England. Their faithful Dundas went with them.

On this journey Anna Josepha kept a journal, which is greatly concerned with her husband's health. At Christmas he was very ill indeed, as he was for a large part of the journey; 'ill in every part' and 'with gout flying about him'. They had taken with them a large tin 'bathing shoe, painted green, big enough to put his whole body into. When he bathes it is placed under the companion outside the cabin door, when it is filled with warm water.' This treatment, twice weekly, helped the gout. 'I often take a dip after him,' she wrote.

It was not a happy voyage. One woman went mad and died, several children and another convict woman died. The master weaver, Mr Wise, was lost overboard, leaving a wife and two children, and the ship's doctor became insane. Small Elizabeth was sick and once had a bad fall. In spite of such happenings Anna stayed reasonably cheerful, and in Cape Town persuaded her husband to stay in port just a little longer to attend a ball. He consented reluctantly and she was delighted, for

> . . . *expecting an amusement of this kind I had provided myself with a dress and therefore had nothing to think of but to recollect my Scotch steps in which, by the bye, I believe I gave my master credit.*

She was glad to have such happy memories for the last part of the voyage, during which there was a split mizzen mast, a fire on board and a tremendous storm that washed away some of the water casks and the Kings' bathing shoe, and flooded cabins, almost submerging Anna and Elizabeth . . . 'it was so dreadful that I thought that any moment we should be lost'.

After eight years away, the Kings found Sydney greatly changed. Government House had been renovated and enlarged and was no longer the only dwelling with a staircase. There were several other imposing buildings and a brick grainstore of three storeys. They could not move in to the house, with its big verandah and pleasant garden running down to the sea, because Governor Hunter took the news of his replacement badly and decided to stay until the ship *Buffalo* was refitted to take him back to England. Fortunately the Patersons were in town, he as Colonel of the New South Wales Corps, and the Kings stayed with them until they could find lodgings.

Hunter finally surrendered his office to King in September 1800. It was all very awkward and the people of Sydney delighted in the plight of departing and incoming Governors. King was appalled at the Sydney scene:

> *Vice, dissipation and a strange relaxation seems to pervade every class and order of people. As to spirits, the cellars are full of that fiery poison. Children are abandoned to misery, prostitution and every vice of their parents. Nothing less than a total change in the system of administration must take place immediately I am left to myself.*

When they were able to move into Government House they found it roomy, if a little dilapidated. The cost of living was high and clothes were difficult to buy. Some of Anna's had been ruined when their cabin was flooded. In the year Elizabeth was 7, she wrote to thank Mr Darcy Wentworth in England for the very pretty bonnet he had procured for her.[4]

The last child, Mary, was born in Sydney in 1805—a fortunate child indeed compared with most of that town's children. There were 958 orphans, most of them children of convict mothers who had been deserted by the fathers—soldiers or sailors. Both the Kings were most concerned. 'Finer or more neglected children are not to be met with in any part of the world,' the Governor said. On Norfolk Island he had started an orphanage, and now he did the same in Sydney. It was in one of the finest buildings in town, built in 1798 for

Lieutenant Kent and surrounded by gardens and orchards. Governor King bought the house for £1539, to be used as a girls' home. Anna Josepha King, Australia's first First Lady, also became its first 'committee lady'. With the help of Mrs Paterson, two clergymen—the Reverend Richard Johnson and the Reverend Samuel Marsden—and surgeons John Harris and William Balmain she supervised the affairs of the orphanage, often called 'Mrs King's Orphanage'. She and Mrs Paterson were in and out of the home every day. Mrs King's hope was that the girls could all be trained to earn their own livings, her dearest wish that they should leave the home to marry honest working men. When she left the country in 1807 she had been stand-in parent at many orphans' weddings and she was sometimes called, though with affection, 'Mrs King, the marriage-broker'.

In her own house she was fortunate for there, always to be relied upon, was the invaluable Jane Dundas. Jane had been with them since they first went to Norfolk Island and had lived with them ever since, in England and now in Sydney. As the Government House housekeeper, 'Mrs' Dundas had become an important and well-known personage.

King made trouble for himself by trying to control the vast trafficking in spirits, mainly by officers of the Corps. John Macarthur, one of whose objects in life seemed to be the bringing down of Governors, was a continual menace and caused bitterness that led to coolness between Anna and her friend Elizabeth Macarthur; to troubles, too, between Kings and Patersons. Both friendships were later resumed.

Although appointed as Governor for five years, King's troubles and gout both persisted and he thought it time to ask to be relieved. Their departure was delayed first by King's illness; then the Hawkesbury grain crops were devastated by floods, which meant their ship, the *Buffalo*, might have to sail to the Cape for supplies. The new Governor, Bligh, arrived and the Kings behaved perfectly by moving out to Government House in Parramatta. Here Anna acted as secretary and took down letters dictated by her husband, who called her 'my under-secretary'. Malicious gossips joked about her strong-mindedness, calling her 'Queen Josepha'.

They sailed in February 1807. The voyage back to England was not easy. Anna often had to act as nurse to her sick husband and they were all disturbed by the request of Mrs Short, who died on the trip, that her body be preserved and taken to England. Mrs King wrote: 'The only way was to put her in a cask of pickle'. Unfortunately she could not be put in whole, and Anna reflected that she herself would prefer a watery grave and would not much care what happened to her body, provided it all went together!

Life was very uncertain for them back in England. King was only 49, but too ill to work any more. His £1000 per year salary had stopped the day Bligh took command, and with his naval half-pay and small investments he had only £220 per year. He asked for a government pension, visited his old friend Admiral Arthur Phillip in Bath, and died in London on 3 September 1808.

Anna Josepha, a widow of 43, petitioned the Secretary of State and at length was granted a life pension of £200 per year, but lost her widow's pension of £80 per year. Maria married Hannibal Hawkins Macarthur (nephew of John) and returned to Sydney with him. Anna's son Phillip, back from naval service in the Mediterranean, also wanted to return to Sydney. She longed to go back too and, having been granted some land by Governor Macquarie, wrote to arrange for a house to be built for her.

Events seemed to conspire against her. Although Phillip married and went to New South Wales and her youngest daughter Mary was also there with her husband Robert Lethbridge (brother of Phillip's wife Harriet), Anna did not return until fifteen years later. The elderly, bonnetted lady who was welcomed 'with a suitable equipage' by Hannibal Macarthur of Parramatta was very different from the 26-year-old girl who had enjoyed picnics on the grass and outings on the water, but her old friend Elizabeth Macarthur found her 'very little changed and as gay as ever'.

Her last years were happy ones, spent in the beautiful house of Maria, now an invalid and mother of eleven. Although Elizabeth had married a widower and lived in London, Anna had three married children and twenty-six grandchildren close by. The Vineyard was a vast and lively estate, filled with people and entertainments of all kinds. Emmeline, Maria's youngest child, when an old lady herself wrote some memories of her grandmother: 'I can see her now, always handsomely dressed and generally wearing an embroidered apron and some white lace or embroidery on her shoulders, quite a picture'.

Phillip Parker King, commander of the *Adventure* and *Beagle* survey expeditions, was elected Fellow of the Royal Society. He retired, as a rear-admiral, to a property across the river from his sister. His seven sons, with all the other grandchildren, were frequent visitors to their 'stately old grandmother'. She died at Parramatta, in her eightieth year, on 26 July 1844. She was buried in St Mary's at South Creek, a church built on land that her son had given, at her request.

The many, many descendants of Anna Josepha have reason to be proud of her. There seems to be no record of her ever having been mean, spiteful or uncharitable, nor was she too good to be true. She was a responsible, intelligent and stout-hearted woman who did an excellent job as Australia's first First Lady.

Mary Reibey

GIRL ON A HORSE — MARY REIBEY

Rich, respectable Mary Reibey[1], widowed since her early thirties, had removed herself in 1850 from the noise and scurry of Sydney town. She built herself a big house in extensive grounds at Newtown, still quiet and countrified. She filled it with fine furniture and had servants to perform all inside and outside duties, allowing her time to sit on committees and do other charity work. She kept a carriage, gave quiet tea parties, attended charity functions.

A plump, small, elderly lady in a lace cap, she looked like a comfortable little Mother Hubbard, but it was many, many years since her cupboard had been at all bare. She was a shrewd, extremely successful business woman who owned properties in the town, farms along the Hawkesbury River, a shipping line, cottages here and there. Her children had married well and her grandchildren were bright and well-educated, fitting easily into polite society.

Mary Reibey was held in high public regard, her advice on business matters and building sought after, her experience in both being wide. In 1829 the *Sydney Gazette* had reported that

> Mrs Reibey, with a perseverance and spirit of enterprise which truly astonished us, having erected many elegant and substantial buildings in Macquarie Place near the Kings Wharf and in the centre of George Street, had now turned her attention towards the improvement of Castlereagh Street, where a noble pile of buildings will soon ornament that hitherto neglected part of the capital.[2]

At that time Mary had owned some of the best property in town. When her youngest daughter Elizabeth married Adjutant Joseph Long Innes in May 1829, she made them a present of a large block of land in George Street. Eighteen years later she bought back from her son-in-law the land on which the Sydney General Post Office now stands.

The genteel and ladylike mien presented to the public by the widow Reibey occasionally cracked. She would appear in the Domain, alone in her carriage drawn by an excellent pair of horses, driving them at a gallop through the park. By a government decree all carriages were 'to proceed at a walking pace', but Mrs Reibey felt she had earned the right to drive as she pleased and when she had the reins in her hands it was the young girl Mary Haydock who stirred up the horses.

There was gossip about Mrs Reibey—not about her morals (which were impeccable) or her business acumen (which was undoubted)—but about her past. She had come to the colony as a convict. People still told stories about that but nobody, after such a long time, knew the truth of it. Only Mrs Reibey herself could have told the true story of her conviction, but she never did. She bent the truth a little at times, as in the 1828 census when, against her name, she had written 'Come free, 1821, the *Mariner*'.[3]

It was the truth in part, for she had been on a year's trip to England. She had returned to Sydney a free, fare-paying passenger, back from visiting England for the first time since she had left it as a convict girl of 15, one of the youngest of the forty-seven women being transported on the *Royal Admiral*.[4]

When the *Royal Admiral*, seventeen weeks out from England, dropped anchor on 7 October 1792, Sydney, four years old, still looked more like a camp than a town. The little settlement hugged the shore of the cove and the banks of the Tank Stream, where a log bridge already in need of repair separated the east and western parts. The stream, first seen as a lively, tree-fringed run of clear water, had changed. Tanks had been let down into its bed to hold drinking water, and with constant use and misuse the muddied stream had lost its beauty.

The dark hills behind were covered with strange trees and along the foreshores, built between rock and scrub, were rows of wattle-and-daub huts, tents, a few small houses, the soldiers' barracks and a hospital and a gaol. Tree-stumps tripped careless feet and pigs rooted through straggling gardens. On the eastern side, the cottages of officials and the Governor's little house stood, with a strip of grass running down to the water in front: solid buildings in a temporary-seeming soldiers' town.

Mary or Molly (her christened name) Haydock was a lively girl, of good education and worthy family—English yeomen who had lived in the same district for many generations. She was born in Bury in May 1777 and lived later with her grandmother, her father having died when she was two. She was a high-spirited and 'rompish' girl, allowed a good deal of freedom by her loving grandmother and considered to be a tomboy by some of the neighbours. It was rumoured amongst them that she sometimes dressed in boys clothes and called herself James.

The rumour was completely true, but it was not generally known until the early 1980s that not only had the girl dressed herself as a boy but had actually been arrested, convicted, sentenced and gaoled as a youth called James Burrow (Burroughs).[5] The charge was that of stealing a horse, a most serious crime in an England where a horse was a most valuable property representing transport, farm labour and gentlemanly sport. A horse was more highly regarded than the life of a servant who could easily be replaced, almost free. Horse-stealing was punishable by hanging, so when in August 1791 a 14-year-old boy called James Burrow offered a stolen horse for sale to two men on the road near Chester, retribution was quick. The thief was gaoled and later tried and convicted. And the thief was Mary Haydock, who had run away from home after her grandmother's death, adopting the disguise and the name of a boy who had died two years earlier.

Five witnesses had sworn and signed their names to the truth of the charge against James Burrow, Labourer of the Parish of Saint Mary, of having stolen and led away, 'against the peace of our said Lord the King, a Bay Mare of his price of Ten Pounds'. The prisoner was found guilty, sentence of hanging was pronounced and the young thief led back to the crowded and stinking gaol. There, by disguise and by the guts which would later inform every action of Mary Reibey, she survived for four and a half months more the dangers of assault and sexual harassment. A small, undeveloped figure, loose workman's smock and shorn hair would have added credibility to the disguise.

Before prisoners were taken to the ships they had to undergo thorough cleansing and reclothing and finally Mary gave in, announced her sex and appealed for family help. A petition dated 5 November 1791, arranged by one of her relatives and signed by respectable members of the home community—tradesmen, merchants, the Reverend Headmaster of the Free Grammar School and one Robert Smalley, Gentleman—was forwarded to the trial judge, the boy James Burrow being now identified as the girl Mary Haydock. Part of the petition reads:

> . . . *a poor helpless orphan prevailed upon by another young girl to leave her situation in the month of June last [1791], to purchase boy's clothing and to change the name Mary Haydock then assuming the name of James Burrow* . . .
>
> . . . *it does not appear that she had any hand in the original Act of stealing the horse* . . . *she was drawn in by the wicked contrivance of some evil-minded person* . . . *it appears still more unlikely that*

she alone could have formed a scheme so daring as that of stealing a Horse.

A local minister, the Reverend Thomas Harkie, forwarded the petition to the Secretary of State and stated that 'her relations in this town are very respectable people and I hope her extreme youth will entitle her to the Royal Mercy'. He did not personally sign the paper as 'not knowing the young girl personally I could not with propriety put my name to it . . .'

After much deliberation Mr Justice Heath rejected the claim of 'perfect innocence' and the placing of blame upon others. However, had any respectable person been willing to act as her guardian and guarantor of behaviour for five years, Mary could have gone free and thus forfeited her future in Australia. No uncle, aunt or cousin was prepared to do so and she was returned to Stafford Prison to await the ship's sailing in April 1792.

This is a more stirring, gritty and dramatic story than the accepted legend, which began to form itself around Mary Reibey during her lifetime and to which she herself certainly contributed. A convict background was not a thing to be flaunted in early Australia and Mary, who bent the truth of her origin in 1828 with the words 'Come free, 1821', must have earlier turned it inside out by conjuring for her children the heart-rending tale of the madcap 13-year-old girl who took a ride on a neighbour's horse, returned it overblown and sweating to the angry owner, and was not given a scolding or simple punishment but was arrested for horse-stealing, imprisoned and transported. The new story is also more logical in its beginnings. The legend gave rise to novels and plays and innumerable articles and Mary would have enjoyed these as greatly as she was to enjoy her comfortable old age in her Newtown house.

The first step towards that prosperity was marriage in September 1794, when she was 17, to Thomas Raby (later changed to Reibey). This young officer with the East India Company had come to the colony as junior officer with Captain Raven on the ship *Britannia*. He acted completely against social custom in applying for permission to marry a convict girl, but then took leave of his ship and the sea for a while and applied for a land grant along the Hawkesbury River. He took his new wife to his new farm and, having profited from trading goods bought during the passage from England, he was able to put some capital into the land. Thomas was not, though, a farmer at heart; he was a sailor and a businessman and knew more money would be made in town. He returned to Sydney with Mary and their son Thomas, born in 1796, and they opened a store in their first house at The Rocks, the craggy sandstone hill on the western side of the cove. Already the area had a bad name. Its narrow alleys and 'rows' were dark and dirty, lined with drinking shops and gambling dens, pig-pens and sailors' brothels.

Thomas went back to sea. There were big profits in shipping and trading, as much as 100 per cent, sometimes 500 per cent. Until 1798 only government officials (including army officers) were allowed to buy goods direct from ships and soon Thomas had his own ship, the *Raven*, which he took up the coast to Newcastle, to trade in timber and coal and later in the cedar being cut along the Hunter River. While he was at sea Mary ran the business and by the end of 1803 the Rabys were growing rich.

In partnership with Mr Edward Wills, Thomas had three schooners which traded up the coast and also south to Bass Strait for sealskins. The house at The Rocks was too small to hold the growing business and the growing family and they moved to Macquarie Place, to a large, two-storey stone house almost on the waterfront. Entally House (named by Thomas after a place he had known in Calcutta) was over 15 metres long and 9 metres high, with grainstores and outhouses behind.[6] By 1807 Thomas and Edward were trading in the Pacific Islands and clever, capable Mary was busy with family and business. She had several assigned servants to help in house and store, but kept accounts herself and found time to give lessons to the children, who had a nursemaid called Fee-Foo, brought back by Captain Raby from Tahiti. By 1810, when her seventh child was born, Mary was one of the busiest women in Sydney. In the early days she had sometimes made a short coastal trip with Thomas, but now the older boys went to sea with their father while Mary managed the business. She was known widely for her acumen and her sometimes hard bargaining.

The family name was now spelled as Reibey (sometimes Reiby or Reibie). The children, who lived on the second floor of the warehouse, could see from their windows the ships of the world coming and going. Sydney had changed. The old rows of huts had been replaced by white-painted cottages with gardens; Simeon Lord, former convict turned merchant prince, had built himself a stone mansion on the waterfront; and on the fringes of the town were some great houses and estates.

In October 1810 Thomas returned from a trip to China and India still ill from a sunstroke he had suffered in India. He died, aged 42, early in April 1811. His partner, Edward Wills, died a few weeks later.

Mary had loved Thomas deeply and valued the position which marriage with him had made possible. She was only 34, a rich widow with seven children, with ships, farms and a warehouse to look after. Young Thomas, just 15, had made several trips with his father and hoped to captain his own ship; James, almost 13, felt the same way about the sea. George was 11, Celia 10; Eliza and Jane Penelope came next and then there was baby Elizabeth. There was little time for tears.

Life became easier for emancipists like Mary after Governor Lachlan Macquarie arrived in Sydney. He admired them and thought that the past should be forgotten. He considered Mary a quite outstanding woman and she was sometimes a guest at Government House.

In July 1811 Mrs Reibey advised in the *Sydney Gazette*[7] that she intended to move her business to No. 12 George Street. She moved there, and later let Entally House to the Bank of New South Wales at £150 per year. When she applied for her first land grant in 1812, 812 hectares near Camden, the Governor granted the request and the land became Toad Hill Farm.

Mary's son Thomas was captain of the *Governor Macquarie*, taking it to Tasmania, where Reibey's Wharf was the first solid one to be built at Launceston. There was a Reibey warehouse there too. Thomas married Richarda Allen, daughter of Dr

Allen who had attended King George in England, and later built not far from Launceston a big stone house which he called Entally. James, though he spent most of his life at sea, also had a land grant—near Hobart—and George, too, lived in Tasmania.

Mary began to feel she could take life more easily. She took her two older girls to England to show them something of the world and give them some English schooling. She would also show herself to people in England as a wealthy widow, a woman of influence who was known and trusted by friends in high places. The relatives who had refused assistance or shelter to the disgraceful boy-girl convict were delighted to welcome her now to their homes. Mary was sometimes quite overcome with the joy of acceptance and of being back in England, but Sydney was her home and after seeing the sights, taking the girls to Scotland and having their portraits painted, she visited warehouses to order goods and decided to return. Eliza, who was to have attended a finishing school in Glasgow, went with her, and soon after returning to Sydney announced her engagement to Lieutenant Thomas Thomson.

For the first time Mary found herself a social figure in Sydney. She had sold or leased some of the properties, was rich and well known, had two pretty, grown-up daughters and two agreeable younger ones. There were two weddings to arrange. Eighteen-year-old Celia was married to Thomas Wills, son of her father's partner, and Eliza to Lieutenant Thomson. Before the festivities Mary had visited Tasmania to see the new Entally House and meet her first grandson, the third Thomas Reibey. For a while, finding the George Street premises now too big, Mary lived in a cottage near the Tank Stream. She took a lively interest in charity work, in church and schools and town planning. Her last move was to the big house at Newtown where she could keep her carriage and stable her horses in comfort and grow old in the same style.

In 1846 the publication of a book in England brought a fresh storm of gossip raging around her head. It was a life of Margaret Catchpole by the Reverend Richard Cobbold and purported to be the 'true story' of a convict woman transported for stealing a horse. Although Margaret Catchpole had died in

1819, people confused her with the respectable Mrs Reibey. Mary was so upset that she asked the help of the Bishop of Tasmania in clearing her name.

That the stigma of a convict past was hard to evade is attested by a letter from Lady Jane Franklin, wife of Tasmania's second Governor, to her sister in London, concerning a proposed visit there by Mr James Reibey:

> . . . there is also a family of the name of Reibey, pronounced Raby, which consists of Mr and Mrs Thomas Reibey of Entally near Launceston, their two boys and their daughter who is married to Mr Charles Arthur, a nephew of Colonel Arthur. Besides them, there is Mr James Reibey, brother of the above and his wife. This gentleman is almost dead of the gout and will scarcely get through the voyage. Mr Thomas R. is one of the biggest landed proprietors in the island and appears to be a good-natured sort of man. He is ambitious and would like to be knighted. This might be a liability to you. Those who know their origin could hardly fail to think so. The mother is said to have been transported to Sydney for horse-stealing and now lives in affluence, driving a phaeton with two white ponies through the streets . . . the daughter Mrs Charles Arthur, a native of the colony, is a very pretty young woman and has a quiet and modest demeanour which distinguishes most of the young families of the island (she is what is vulgarly called a Currency Lass) but in spite of her beauty and her father's riches, I cannot conceive that the Arthur family would have been satisfied with the match.[8]

That daughter was Mary Ellen, and her two brothers, Thomas (III) and James were educated in England and both became clergymen. Thomas, who took over Entally House when his father died, became Archdeacon of Launceston. He later went into politics and for twelve months was Premier of Tasmania. He was also a well-known racehorse breeder and when he died in February 1912, at the age of 91, he was the last male to carry the Reibey name.

Two of Mary's children died early, the pretty Celia only fifteen months after her marriage in June 1822 to Thomas Wills, 'to whom she bequeathed a pledge of their tenderest affections—a sweet little girl'. George, 23 and still single, was killed in an accident while 'fowling'. These deaths were perhaps the saddest part of growing old for Mary, who was still rich and busy with visits and regular letters from grandchildren to keep her in touch with family affairs. She held the family reins as firmly as she held the horses' reins when she galloped through the park.

Sydney now was nothing like the little rough place Mary had first known, a place of rock and scrub and bark huts, chain-gangs and the sound of reveille on drum and fife. It had a population of 53 000 and streets of fine buildings, some of which had been to her own credit. She lived there, in the town she loved, for sixty-three years. She died on 30 May 1855 and was buried beside Thomas.

Margaret Catchpole

'LIK A LADEY'

1803:

> i am well Beloved by all that know me and that is a Comfrt for i all wais Goe into better Compeney than Myself that is a monkest free peopell when they make much of me as if i was a Lady—Because i am the Cominissires Cook. P.S. i have at this time a man that keep me compeney and would marrey me if i lik But i am not for marring he is a Gardner he Com out as a Botnes and to Be a Lowed one Hundred pound per year and one to go with him to collect Sides [seeds] and Skines [skins] and all kinds of curosites.[1]

The spelling was rude and original and full of life. Margaret Catchpole, convict, was uneducated but intelligent and determined. She had taught herself to write and read by sitting in on lessons with the Cobbold children, to whom she was nursemaid. She wrote words as she heard them, the accents of England sounding back in her own Suffolk ears. Her spiky letters, homesick for England, illuminate a tough era in the colony of New South Wales—life as it was lived by very ordinary people.

Margaret never did marry, a quite extraordinary retreat from female custom and convenience when women were so much in the minority that to refrain from marriage or an 'arrangement' signified an unusually forceful character.

1806:

> *I myself will hev no husband though hear is no women But have sum sort of man, sum women do very well indeed. I might a gon to lived with a manny of the sailors that is to be their wife and might have lived very well but i hav no inclinashon.*

She was writing to her uncle and aunt in England, assuring them:

> *I don't know any want, Bless God, for i have Benn nurse to Lying in women and i will take that kear I will not want, it is a great word to say but I am well Beloved amongst my Betters i never have knowen one thing of punishment since i have been hear only that I cannot get no tea.*

Was she too pleased with herself? Was it the satisfaction of being so well treated by her betters that kept her single? She was not vain of her appearance, but of her achievement of respectability so soon after arrival as a convict. A plain, sallow-skinned, strong-featured woman, she gives, in some letters, a hint of masculinity which might have accounted for her decision to stay in charge of her own life.

Margaret Catchpole is a unique figure among Australia's convict women. Twice sentenced to death, twice reprieved and once a notorious escapee, she arrived in Sydney on the *Nile* in December 1801. Captain Sunter and Surgeon Hislop had kept strict hygiene rules, so that every one of the ninety-six women convicts arrived in reasonable health. They had been taken on deck daily for fresh air; bottom boards had been removed from berths twice weekly, taken up, scrubbed with salt water and dried. Their quarters, barred cells 3·6 metres square, had been fumigated regularly, as had clothing of hospital cases.

Good behaviour early established, Margaret had cooked meals for some of the free settlers on board and acted as midwife for another. In the clouded waters of Australian history legends formed about her, as they did about Mary Reibey. It is unlikely that the two met. By the time Margaret came, Mary Reibey and her Tom were well established in warehouse and shipping trade; Mary had several children, had proved herself as competent in domestic affairs as in business and was fast acquiring her reputation as Sydney's most successful business woman.

The two were sometimes confused, though the only thing they shared was a conviction for horse-stealing. After the publication of the Reverend Richard Cobbold's[2] novel, *The History of Margaret Catchpole, a Suffolk Girl*, rumours spread around Sydney that the rich widow Reibey, eminently respectable, was really Margaret Catchpole, notorious horse-thief. Mary's own past history had by then been well camouflaged and almost forgotten and she asked the Bishop of Tasmania to help clear her name. The Bishop's firm, admonitory letter was published in a second edition of the book.

Claiming to be 'the true history', the Catchpole story was as romanticised and fictive as it was successful. It was a bestseller and people flocked to see a play based on it, a 'spectacle' which managed to reproduce on stage the Hawkesbury River in flood.

Margaret had worked for Cobbold's mother for many years as housemaid, cook and nurse. Her letters to Mrs Cobbold and to her uncle and aunt Leader are among the Mitchell and National Library treasures today and tell a different tale from the polished version offered by Cobbold. 'The heroine of this romantic but perfectly true narrative', he wrote, 'was born in the year 1773'. She was already 11 years old then, the youngest child of Jonathon Catchpole, head ploughman at Priory Farm near Ipswich. As a small girl she was often in the fields with her father, perched on the vast back of a Suffolk Punch carthorse. She loved horses, was an excellent rider and once made a wild and difficult mercy ride to the nearest town to fetch Dr Stebbings to the epileptic wife of a farmer, a ride which made a local legend.

Cobbold made various romances for her and had her meet again, in Australia, a faithful admirer, marry him, become rich, produce children and even return to her Suffolk village in triumph. At the time he was writing of this marriage Margaret was telling her relatives: 'my eyes are not so good as they were. I do not grow young myself for I have lorst all my frunt teeth'! The next year, 1812, she wrote: 'March the 14th is my Barthday, then i am fiftey years old'.

The letter quoted by Cobbold, supposedly written to his mother on 25 June 1812, was to thank her for goods she no longer needed.

> . . . because God has blessed me with such abundance. Everything I could wish for, and oh! how much more than I deserve, have I had granted to me in this place of probation! Dearest lady, I have menservants and maid-servants, horses and cattle, flocks and herds in abundance. I have clothing and furniture above what you can imagine and a house wide enough to entertain in it all your numerous family. But more than all this, I have an excellent husband, one whose constancy from his youth has been beyond the praise I could find language to express.

Finally, Cobbold provided Margaret with a son and two daughters, who received the best education England could supply and returned to live rich, distinguished, outstanding lives in their native land. After the death of this loving husband, and having inherited all his property, Cobbold's Margaret lived in Sydney in unostentatious style and died there in 1841, aged sixty-eight.

The real Margaret Catchpole had then been dead for twenty-two years. The ordinariness of her life in Australia was attested by the fact that her death went unremarked in the *Sydney Gazette*. There was no mention of the passing of a woman who had once occupied the headlines in English newspapers and about whom a public notice had been posted:

> March 16 1800
>
> # ESCAPED
>
> **FROM THE COUNTY GAOL IPSWICH**
>
> Last Night or early this Morning
>
> # MARGARET CATCHPOLE A CONVICT
>
> Twice Sentenced for Transportation for
>
> **FELONY & HORSE STEALING**
>
> She is about 38 years of age, Swarthy Complexion — very dark eyes and hair
> Escaped in a convict's dress which she had probably changed & may be disguised in *Men's Apparel*
>
> **WHOEVER SHALL APPREHEND THIS MARGARET CATCHPOLE**
> So she may be brought to Justice Will be entitled to a Reward of
>
> **TWENTY POUNDS**
>
> Granted by Act of Parliament

The truth of the bill is undoubted. It was already in print and on display by the time the horse-thief reached London, after an extraordinary ride of 112 kilometres from Ipswich in eight and a half hours. She was apprehended and returned to gaol.

It is impossible to verify the tale told of the reason for her escape and for her original imprisonment, but it is such a satisfyingly romantic story that it *deserves* to be truth.

The key figure was a sailor called William Laud, with whom Margaret Catchpole was in love. She had known him since she was 15 and the handsome, blue-eyed sailor was then working in the boatbuilding trade with his father, who ran a ferry at Felixstowe. They 'kept company' for many years, but Will kept bad company too. He became a notorious smuggler and came and went from her life.

Margaret worked at the Priory Farm for Mrs Cobbold for many years, as nursemaid, housekeeper, cook and trusted family retainer. She was devoted to her mistress, a generous, religious and busy matriarch with half a dozen children and a large family from Mr John Cobbold's first marriage. If Margaret dreamed of Will and marriage, they were unfulfilled dreams. He had become an honest sailor again and, after being 'pressed' into the navy, earned a good share of prize money for bringing back to port a captured French ship. He vanished again.

Margaret, now in her thirties, became moody and difficult. She quarrelled with her mistress and took work elsewhere, stayed with her loved aunt and uncle, with her father, with friends.

The element of fiction is surely woven into the meeting in an Ipswich street with a former acquaintance, bearing a message from Laud. She was to join him in London, having first stolen a horse to ride there and sell for ready money.

She did steal a horse from the Cobbold stables and, dressed in groom's clothes, made the furious ride to London which led to her imprisonment in Newgate Gaol and then in Ipswich.

Margaret Catchpole was tried at the Summer Assizes in Bury St Edmonds in 1798. Horse-stealing was a heinous crime and the town buzzed with the news of a woman criminal. A speech she made in her own defence impressed the judge, and evidence of good character was given by Mr Cobbold, by Dr

STOLEN

Out of the Stables of JOHN COBBOLD, ESQ. of St Margaret's Green in this Town, late last Night or early this Morning, with a Saddle

STRAWBERRY ROAN CROP COACH GELDING SIX OR SEVEN YEARS OLD

With a Black Main and nag Tail; about 16 Hands and a half High . . .

A man was seen riding Horse answering to above Description about 3 o'clock this Morning on the Road towards London, 2 Miles this side Colchester.

£50 offered for Information

Stebbing (who had known her as a child) and by her uncle and aunt. She had never been in trouble, but because of the crime's seriousness sentence of death was passed, later commuted to transportation.

A model prisoner, Margaret was soon put on special duties by Mr Ripshaw, head warder. After two years she made a spectacular escape, scaling a 6·7 metre spiked wall with a rope clothes-line taken from the laundry where she was working, and using a wooden clothes-horse as a stand. The reason for her escape was rumoured to be that she had heard from Laud, who would meet her on the coast road whence they would escape to France and quit England for ever.

She did leave for ever—alone. In a fight with waiting coastguards Laud, it was said, had been shot dead. Margaret was returned to prison, tried for a second time and again sentenced to death. A second reprieve meant transportation for life. In absolute misery at the thought of leaving England she appealed to friends and wrote to Mrs Cobbold, who visited her in prison, taking her money, books, clothes and a collection of useful things like pins, needles and cottons. On 21 June 1801 Margaret sailed on the *Nile* and arrived in Sydney on 14 December.

Good behaviour on board ship could have been responsible for her quick assignment as servant to Mrs Palmer, wife of the good-natured, jolly little John Palmer, a First-Fleeter, now Commissary-General of New South Wales.[3] Wooloomooloo House, which Palmer had built on his 100 acre (40·5 hectare) land grant, was large and handsome and well-furnished, one of the grandest houses in Sydney. Its wide gardens ran down to the harbour; its ornamental gates opened to admit the carriages of the best people in town, for the Palmers entertained sumptuously.

Now Margaret Catchpole felt that her life had turned a most comfortable corner. She gave the same kind of devoted service to the charming Mrs Palmer as she had to Mrs Cobbold. The Commissary's cook delighted in her good position, revelled in her fortune and was pleased indeed when ladies who had dined deliciously asked for permission to present their compliments to the cook. 'They treat me quite as though i am a Ladey myself.' She was very proud of it. Mrs Palmer was an American who had married her husband in New York when he was with the British navy during the American War of Independence. Democratic, good-natured, she valued highly the competence of her new cook.

Margaret longed for England. She wrote many letters and felt forgotten when there were no replies. To Mrs Cobbold she wrote thanking her for kindness during troubled days, adding:

> . . . *not that i am myself troubell now but hear is manney a one that have their poor head shaved and sent up the Cook River and thear to carrey Coales from Day light till Dark at Night and half starved but i hear that is going to be put by and so it had for it is a cruwell thing and Norfolk Island is a bad place to send any poor creatur.*

Suitors came calling on the Commissary's cook—sailors, soldiers, a widower farmer with several children and in need of a new wife, and the government 'botness'—a gardener who was to collect specimens for England. He was once thought to be the well-known George Caley, but Caley, a protégé of Sir Joseph Banks, had applied for permission to marry a young widow with two children who had travelled out on the same ship and whose husband had died on the voyage. The 'botness' was more likely James Gordon, sent to the colony by Mr J. A. Woodford of the War Office.

Happy though she was with the Palmers, Margaret hankered for the country. She left them and worked as live-in midwife and nurse for a while for Mrs Samuel Skinner, whose husband had a china shop and small factory in Pitts Row (Pitt Street). Eventually she went to Richmond to help Mrs Rouse, for whom she had been midwife on the voyage. Life in the Hawkesbury River district suited her and there was more work than she could do. There were many farms along the river and a new baby almost yearly for each family meant that wives regularly needed the services of a good nurse and midwife.

Richard and Elizabeth Rouse had created Oxford Farm on a 100 acre (40·5 hectare) grant made in 1802. There were three children already and babies continued to arrive until there were seven living of the nine born. Margaret was regarded as a second mother—and finally, grandmother—to them all. She was also adopted into the Dight family and became closely attached to Hannah Dight, wife of another free settler. Living in both these houses widened her experience of farming and later she rented a cottage and started her own small farm. She grew herbs and brewed potions and salves for her continuing work as district nurse. At one time she also opened a shop in her front room.

When Richard Rouse was made Superintendent of Public

Works at Parramatta, and moved there, Margaret stayed at Oxford Farm as overseer, but found it too lonely and went back to her own place. She now had four ewes, nine breeding goats, three wethers and seven lambs. She was with the Dights during the disastrous Hawkesbury floods of 1810 and sought refuge with Hannah and the children in the loft while the water lapped close to the ceiling just below. When it was safe to come down she took part in days of rescue work. As a result of constantly being immersed in water she was very ill afterwards, weak and listless; the strength she was so proud of seemed to have gone. It was restored by the arrival of the first letters from England, better than any tonic, more valuable than a fortune to the homesick woman.

Health was restored, energy returned. She made more friends of the kind that further increased her opinion of her own worth, for she was now accepted as trusted employee and friend by the Pitt family at Bronte Homestead. Mrs Pitt's first cousin was married to a sister of Admiral Lord Nelson and Margaret warmed her self-esteem in this distant glory.

Towards the end of 1810 she had news that a box of goods sent her from England had been waiting in Sydney for some months. She *walked* to town to collect them:

> Dear uncl you must think I can walk well for i heard thear was a Box for me and i set off and walked fiftey miles in the 2 days you cannot tell the happnes it give me and all my friends wear joyed to hear it . . . I do not grow young myself for i hav lorst all my frunt teeth but i can stir about as Brisk as ever and in good spirits.

Previously she had written of being 'in charmen health but a good manney of my teeth is broken away and all my hopes is to see you and my dear Cussones agen'.

She was always proud of leading an honest, decent and industrious life. 'I am liven all a loan as Before in a very onest way of life thear is no woman in the coloney liv lik myself.'

In 1814 Margaret was granted a pardon by Governor Lachlan Macquarie. She was 52 years old and had lost most of her teeth, but boasted in letters of being 'as struwen and numble as ever', that she was at a loss in no part of the world 'for I am as supell as ever and they say i am lik a young woman for struwen and numble' (strength and nimbleness).

She needed both when a call came, in May 1819, to help the Pitt family, stricken with influenza at Bronte Homestead. She nursed them all to health, then went to tend the old sick shepherd in his hut, visiting daily in wet, windy weather which made her joints ache and her 'struwen and numble' fade. She caught influenza herself and had no strength to fight it. She died, and was buried in St Peter's churchyard in Richmond, recorded by the Reverend Henry Fulton as 'Margaret Catchpole, 58 years, came a prisoner in the Nile in the year 1801, died May 13, was buried May 14, 1819'.[4]

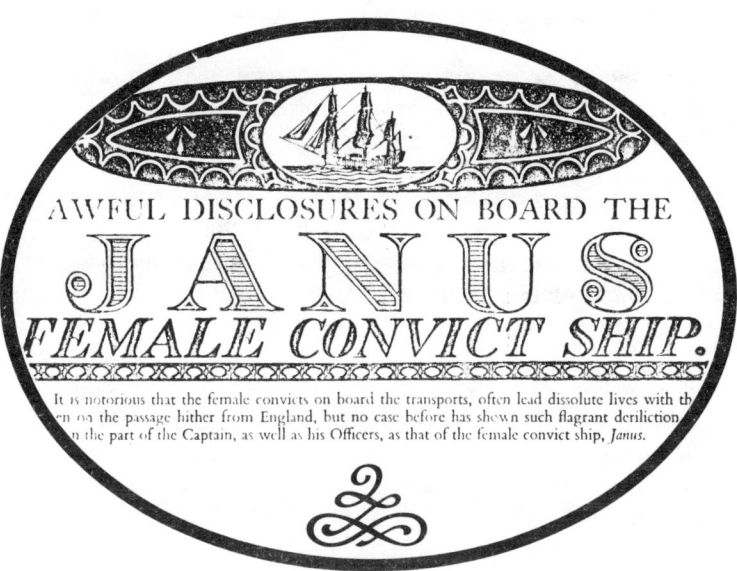

Heading from Sydney Broadsheet, 1820

LETTERS FROM WOMEN

The 'Ladies' of colonial Australia who came from educated families were provided with an excellent tool against loneliness or boredom. They could write long letters home for relatives and friends to cherish and to tuck away so that 20th-century eyes would take pleasure and knowledge from them in public libraries and historical journals.

Among the women convicts, however, reading and writing were not common abilities, nor was the lack held against a woman who could sign her name only with a mark or thumb-print. A rare few could write, some self-taught and awkward;

ashamed relatives in England, not knowing these ill-spelled and anguished scrawls were history, often destroyed them. Miraculously, some convict letters survived to illuminate the lives of such women and the country's history.

The real writing skill of Sarah Bird gives a vivid and excellent account of her voyage to Sydney in the 1790s. Sarah lived with her father in Reigate and, at the age of 24, was employed in the house of William Bryan of Westminster. She was a light-fingered maid and on 7 July 1794 her employer found her with a bundle of his property. Nine days later at the Old Bailey she was judged guilty of stealing four silk handkerchiefs valued at 4 shillings, a cotton window curtain, 10 shillings, a linen tablecloth, 6 shillings; sentence: seven years' transportation.

She was one of 133 female convicts who came on a French-built ship, the *Indispensable*, on which conditions were far superior to those on the usual convict ship. She arrived on 30 April 1796 and wrote to her father shortly afterwards. Her letter was published in November 1798 in the *True Briton* as 'Letter from a woman lately transported to Botany Bay to her father'.

> *I take the first opportunity of informing you of my safe arrival in this remote quarter of the world after a pretty good passage of six months. Since my arrival I have purchased a house, for which I gave £20. And the following articles which are three turkies at 15s each; three sucking pigs at 10s; a pair of pigeons at 8s; a yard dog £2; two muscovy ducks at 10s each, three English ducks at 5s each, and a goat, five guineas; six geese, at 15s each. I have got a large garden to the house, and a licence; the sign is 'The Three Jolly Settlers'. I have met with tolerable good success in the public line. I did a little trade in the passage here in a small number of articles, such as sugar, tea, tobacco, thread, snuff, needles and everything that I could get anything by. The needles are a shilling a paper here and fine thread is sixpence a skain. I have sold my petticoats at two guineas each and my long black cloak at ten guineas, which shews that black silk sells well here; the edging that I gave 1s 8d per yard for in England, I got 5s for here. I have sold all the worst of my cloaths, as wearing apparel brings a good price. I bought a roll of Tobacco at Rio de Janiero, of 54-lb weight, which I was cheated out of. It cost me 20s*

and I could have got 12s a pound for it here. I likewise bought a cwt of sugar there, and also many other articles. Rum sells for 1s 6d the gallon there and here at times, £2. Any person coming from England with a few hundred pounds laid out at any of the ports that shipping touch are liable to make a fortune. Shoes that cost 4s or 5s per pair in England will bring 10s to 15s here. On our passage here we buried only two women and two children . . . I live by myself and did not do as the rest of the women did on the passage which was every one of them that could had a husband. I shall conclude with my kind love to my brother and sisters, nieces and nephews, so am, dear father, your ever dutiful and loving daughter till death.   S.B.[1]

A year after her arrival Sarah, obviously an excellent business woman who had come out with some money (probably supplied by her father), had worked hard and earned herself a good reputation. Although not pardoned, she had been given the freedom to work in her own business. Well-behaved convicts were often allowed to do this. In April 1797 Sarah was granted a licence to use her house as an inn, The Three Jolly Settlers.

Alas, her business acumen and hard-headedness deserted her when she met a rascal called John Morris, a convict twelve years older than she, who became her lover. They moved to the Hawkesbury district and in September 1798 Morris was granted a licence to sell spirits at their Highlander Inn. He was bankrupt within a few years and the family (Sarah had two daughters, Sarah and Ann) went to Norfolk Island to try again.

Morris—a natural criminal, it seemed—was soon gaoled for continuing petty crime. Desperate and perhaps mad, at 5 a.m. on 8 January 1804 Morris tried to stab his gaoler, Edward Garth, with a knife he had hidden in his sleeve. He then rushed to Sarah's house, took out his long-bladed knife and cut her throat while she was in bed. Sarah fought violently, also receiving a cut across the arm which severed the wrist sinews. Her screams alerted neighbours, who overpowered Morris. He was locked up and later brutally punished, sentenced to thirty years' hard labour and to reside permanently in New South Wales. He became incorrigible and in May 1819, at Newcastle, he murdered Joseph Mars and was hanged.

Both Sarah and the gaoler recovered from their wounds. She returned to Sydney with her daughters, went back to England for a while, then returned again to the colony as a free settler, opening another small public house. Later she became housekeeper to the government printer, George Howe, a former convict. Her daughter Ann married Howe's son Robert and, after his death, was for a while the proprietor of the newspaper *Sydney Gazette*. Sarah died in 1842, 84 years old.

An early letter, written towards the end of the first year of settlement, shows a more timid spirit:

> *Port Jackson, 14th September, 1788. I take the first opportunity that has been given me to acquaint you with our disconsolate situation in this solitary waste of the creation. Our passage, you may have heard by the first ships, was tolerably favourable; but the inconveniences since suffered for want of Shelter, bedding, etc. are not to be imagined by any stranger. However, we now have two streets, if four rows of the most miserable huts you can possibly conceive deserve that name. Windows they have none, as from the Governor's house, etc. now nearly finished, no glass could be spared; so that lattices of twigs are made by our people to supply their places . . . as for the distresses of the women, they are past description, as they are deprived of tea and other things they were indulged in in the voyage by the seamen, and as they are all totally unprovided with clothes, those who have young children are quite wretched. Besides this, though a number of marriages have taken place, several women who became pregnant on the voyage are since left by their partners, who have returned to England and are not likely even here to form any fresh connections . . . our kangaroo rats are like mutton, but much larger, and there is a kind of chickweed so much like our spinach that no difference in taste can be discerned. Something like ground ivy is used for tea but a scarcity of salt and sugar makes our best meals insipid. The separation of several of us to an uninhabited island [Norfolk] was like a second transportation. In short everyone is so taken up with their own misfortunes that they have no pity to bestow upon others. All our letters are examined by an officer, but a friend takes this for me privately.*[2]

A letter written about the time of the Second Fleet's arrival described a fairly good voyage for 223 women and twelve children, with 'only three women and 1 child' dying.

> Five or six were born on board the ship; they had great care taken of them, baby linen and every necessary. This place was in a starving condition before we arrived and an allowance of only 2 lb of flour and 2 lb salt pork for each man for a week, and these were almost starved and could not work but three hours in the day. They had no heart and the ground won't grow anything, only in parts here and there. There is a place called Rose Hill [Parramatta] about 20 miles from this, where they say there are four cornfields. But it does not grow much wheat. We are now much in want of everything. We have hardly any cloaths, but since the Scarborough, Neptune and Surprise arrived we have had a blanket and a rug given to us and we hope to have some cloaths, as the Justinian, a ship that came from London is bringing some cloth and linen and we are to make the cloaths. Oh! if you had but seen the shocking sight of the poor creatures that came out with those three ships it would make your heart bleed; they were almost dead, very few could stand and they were obliged to fling them as you would goods, and hoist them out of the ships, they were so feeble; and they died ten or twelve a day when they first landed . . . but some of them are getting better. They were not so long as we were in coming here but they were confined and had bad victuals and stinking water. The governor was very angry and scolded the captains a great deal, and, I heard, intended to write to London about it, for I heard him say it was murdering them . . . I don't think I shall get away from this place to come again to see you without an order from England . . . I hope you will try to get an order for me, that I may once more see you all.[3]

In 1820 a letter was written in New South Wales which led to a court case and the publication of a broadsheet, sold in the streets of Sydney, which was headed 'Awful Disclosures on Board the *Janus* Female Convict Ship'.

> It is notorious that the female convicts on board the transports often lead dissolute lives with the seamen on the passage hither from England but no case before has shown such flagrant dereliction of Duty on the part of the Captain, as well as his Officers, as that of the female convict ship, Janus.[4]

The *Janus*, commanded by Captain Thomas J. Mowatt, arrived in Sydney on 3 May 1820. In the usual way, the 104 English and Irish women convicts were distributed around the countryside as servants to married settlers or sent to the

Female Factory. Lydia Esden and Mary Long were sent to a former officer, now landowner, Mr Nicholas Bayly, Esquire, of Bayly Park. Both women were pregnant. Indeed, it was soon apparent that almost *all* the women were pregnant. Lydia and Mary left the Bayly house to try to get to Sydney to see the men responsible, but were accused of absconding and brought back. Lydia explained why they had gone, said they would have returned as soon as possible and asked for two leave passes. These were at first granted, then refused. Bayly said he would write to the Governor on their behalf and Lydia Esden wrote a letter to go with his, as Mary Long could not write. Because Lydia had somehow learned to write, her anguish still has power to disturb us today.

Honoured Sir, My Feelings Is Mutch Hurt At The Disponding News I Heard from you This morning. That of Being Put off with The Passes. As you have given me but Little Hopes After promising me you Woud. Sir! I hope to God you Will Not be Worse than your word; For if so I Never Shall Be Happy. And In Respect to my Conduct During my Absence Hope you have Not So Bad An Opinion Of me, As To Think me So Base As To Treat your Kindness with Ungrattude By Behaviour Ill, Or Not Coming Back to the Time you May Think Proper to Allow me, Sir, I Prommise you Faithfully I will Not Incrouth one Hour, Sir! I Do Not Wish to take Any Rash Steps with Mr Hedges, As He Is Willing To make Acknowledgement, Providing he As Interview with me. The Reason Things was not Settled Before Wee parted was Wee Expected I Should have Being Able to have gone To See him with Out Any truble. And being Wholely Out of his power to Come to Me, makes me To Intreet So Hard for a pass. Sir! If not Intruding, Let me Once more Beg For a Pass to Parramatta, and if I cannot goe any Further, I will send for him to meet me there, Which Will not Hesitate One moment in Executing the Command I know.

Wat makes me So Anchous Is the Ship Is Goeing A Waleing, And I Am Shure He will Not Stay But very Little Longer, As He would Loose the Season for it. Sir! I hope you will Not Denigh me This Request Or I am a Lost Woman. Sir! I have maney Things to say to Him, As he will goe to see my Famley, which will Be Of grate Concolation To me, And Sattisfaction to them. For God sake, Sir, Take It into Concideration, And greant me my Request, Though I Acknowledge It very Early To Ask Favours, Sir, there Seamed To

> *Be a Dought Ariseing Concerning My Being with Child, But I am Not Desceved. It would Be well if I was; Nor Did I Entend To Name; But When you put the question To me, I could not Denigh the Truth. I Hope, Sir, you will grant this request To-morrow Or Tuesday, As Then I should Be Able To Return By the Latter part of the Week, And Help with the work. Your Hum'l Serv't Lydia Esden.*
>
> *Sir, Mary Long most Earnestly Begs you will Not Failed In your promises To Her.*

The passes were refused, being contrary to government orders. Like so many women of the time, Lydia and Mary were left to fend for themselves; to bear and bring up their children as they could and fade away from history. They did not fade away, however, but left shadows behind. Lydia's badly spelled, eloquent letter tells some of her story.

A court case was held and the Captain and his officers found to have been more than negligent (the Captain and the Mate had been responsible for the condition of Lydia and Mary). Indeed, they were found to have taken the lead in the bad behaviour on board ship. They were duly reprimanded—and allowed to go back to sea!

A cheerful, charming little letter from Tasmanian archives tells a happy story of one girl on a ship filled with women brought out as emigrants and possible brides for settlers—one of the ships which had a carefully chosen complement of passengers. The writer, Susan Gale, briefly stands out from history because of her delightful letter with its entirely original spelling. The end of the story is unknown.

> *As soon as the botes rode to land I don't aggrivat the Truth to say there was half a duzzen Bows apiece to Hand us out to shoar and sum go so far as they was offered to thro speeking Trumpets afore they left the shipside. Be that as it may or may not I am tould we maid a Verry pretty site all waulking too and too in our bridle wite gounds with the Union Jacks afore us to pay humbel respex to Kernel Arthur who behaved very gentlemanny and complemented us on our handsum apperance and Pertitely sed he wisht us All in the United States [matrimony!].*

> *The salers was so gallnt as give three cheers wen we left there Ship and sed if so be they had not Bean without Canons they wood have saluted us all round. Servants mite live long enuff in Lonnon without being sich persons of Distinshun. For my hone part cumming among strangers and Pig in Pokes prudence dicktated not to be askt out At the very fust cumming in honesumever All is settled now and the match is approved off by Kernel Arthur and the Brightlish Gevernment what as agreed to give me away. Thems wot I call Honners as we used to say at wist.*[5]

Sweet Susan! Was she as pretty, small and as lively as her letter and was the marriage a happy one?

In the same year, Sarah Thornton wrote a letter to English relatives. Sentence of death in December 1803 had been commuted to life — for stealing lace from a London shop. She had arrived in Sydney in July 1814 on the *Broxhornbury* and her husband Samuel, a tailor by trade, joined her later. By 1818 he had a liquor licence and by 1822 there were five young children and the couple owned twenty head of horned cattle. Sarah was granted a pardon in 1820 and a free pardon five years later. Although they were quite successful, Sarah could not completely accept her life there and tried, in her letter, to warn young women of the dire consequences of bad conduct.

> *Myself and husband have had many hard struggles to gain the means of an honest livelihood. To accomplish it we have worked night and day. I thank God that he has crowned our endeavours with success. I rose early in the morning and went to market bringing home my articles on my head, to furnish my shop to best advantage. With the greatest care of our little profits and the greatest frugality in housekeeping, we collected together enough to buy a little house. I then applied to the Gentlemen of the Colony, for a licence, which they not only granted but said they would assist me and my husband in any way in their power, as they had noticed our industry and that associated with none but persons of good character.*
>
> *Oh that my voice could be heard by young people in England, to deter them from evil ways . . . that they might not come to this wretched country where so much evil abounds. For though I have by a regular line of good conduct and great privations arrived at a state*

of comfort, not one in twenty who is sent here obtains even the necessaries of life by their own industry.[6]

Sarah died at Parramatta in November 1827. Her good example seems to have inspired her children. Her son George, a shipping agent, was Mayor of Sydney in 1853 and 1857, first Mayor of Woollahra, a member of the NSW Legislative Assembly and a Legislative Councillor for twenty-four years.

Louisa Ann Meredith

A WOMAN OF LETTERS

Louisa Anne Twamley was a bluestocking, a young lady of formidable accomplishment, rather more 'clever' than was customary in genteel English society in the 1820s and 1830s. Born in Birmingham in July 1812 and educated mainly at home by her mother, in her early twenties she had published a book, *Poems*, illustrated with her own etchings, followed by *The Romance of Nature* and *The Annual of British Landscape Scenery*. She wrote well, was an able naturalist and excellent artist who enjoyed stimulating company and intelligent conversation.

The lack of this would distress her years later in the colonial society of New South Wales, when she complained that the ladies spoke about scarcely anything other than dress or domestic events and interminably complained about their servants. The gentlemen were equally limited, though in their case the subject was sheep. Their souls could well have been 'felted up', for they spoke of nothing but wools, fleece, flocks and stock. However fascinating his peerless sheep might be, a gentleman, Louisa Anne considered, should not take them out to dinner!

> *I had to endure a perpetuity of mutton in the wool; whilst choice samples tied and labelled with most fond accuracy, were passed from hand to hand and contemplated with the profound and critical air of a connoisseur passing judgement on a masterpiece of art.*[1]

She thought the gentlemen might well be excused for their verbal devotion to sheep (which were making a fortune for many of them) because the ladies' conversation was so limited that the men were entirely thrown back on their own favoured topic.

It is possible that colonial society found Louisa a little intimidating. Her parents, politically-minded, had brought their daughter up to think for herself and express her opinions on the political and social issues of the day. She was interested in everything that went on about her, particularly in plant life and in all creatures feathered, furred or finned, an interest which developed to expert knowledge as she grew older.

When she was 27 this extremely intelligent and lively young woman married her cousin Charles Meredith, a year older than she and recently returned from New South Wales, where he had a sheep property. He had lived in Australia since he was 10, having gone to Tasmania in 1821 with his father and brothers and sisters. There his father took up land and developed the property Cambria. Charles later went to New South Wales and started to build up his own sheep run. Soon after her marriage Louisa was on the way to New South Wales, leaving England early in June 1839 and arriving in Sydney in September. She kept a journal on the voyage which she expanded later to become a book, published in 1844 as *Notes* and *Sketches of New South Wales During a Residence in that Colony from 1839 to 1844.*

It was a most successful book; thousands of English people had relatives in Australia and were avid for news of that distant place. It sold well and there was a new edition in 1861. The girl who had been educated to 'express herself fearlessly' did so in her book. Some of her comments on the behaviour of ladies and gentlemen in New South Wales did not make her popular with those people, but her sharp eye for detail of country, custom, people, nature, landscape 'and the various objects which strike a newcomer as novel or remarkable' make it an excellent and sometimes sparkling record of colonial life.

Life at sea was monotonous and there was not the diversion of regular ports, for the *Letitia* was going direct to Sydney. Louisa kept herself busy with wool embroidery and with long discussions about flying fish, Portuguese men-of-war (she kept these in a bucket to study them), the phosphorescence on the sea at night, a flight of migrating swallows that landed on the rigging, dolphins, stars and waterspouts. To her 'partial' eyes, the stars of the southern hemisphere seemed less splendid than those she had known before.

As the ship passed through the Heads and approached Sydney there was a light shower, and then a rainbow to welcome her to the new world. Louisa was particularly struck by the remarkable *clearness* of atmosphere, the strong light which gave to distant houses, beaches and trees clean and compelling lines which she felt she wanted to paint.

She was delighted to be on land again, to drink and wash with fresh, *clean* water, to have vegetables after a long diet of pork and rice, to see glasses and plates stay still on a table!

At first, Sydney charmed.

> *When you consider that it has risen in little more than fifty years, its size, appearance and population are truly wonderful. In the afternoon, when the ladies of the place drive out, a whole string of carriages may be seen rolling about or waiting near the fashionable emporiums, that being the term in which Australian shopkeepers especially delight.*

> As no lady in Sydney (your grocers' and butchers' wives included) believes in the possibility of walking the various machines upon wheels of all description are very numerous. Few ladies venture to risk their complexions to the exposure of an equestrian costume and so few appear on horseback.[2]

Although she loved the gardens of Sydney, Louisa soon found the town itself tiresome and the heat made her languid and unhappy. Dust and flies and mosquitoes were appalling and in hotel bedrooms she found, too, that there were sometimes bedbugs and always fleas 'which seem to pervade this colony in a universal swarm'. The excellent collection of books available in the 'Australian Library' delighted this committed reader, who thought the circulating libraries were very poor affairs but feared there was little demand for reading, the gentlemen being too busy or preferring a cigar to a book, and the ladies, 'to quote a witty friend, pay more attention to the adornment of their heads *without* than *within*!'. Louisa gladly admitted there were exceptions, but considered that most of the ladies were completely uninterested in anything except gossip. Nobody discussed literature or art or politics, nobody *thought*!

If the new Mrs Meredith made her opinions clear, it was perhaps as well that she was to leave Sydney soon to visit sheep stations with her husband. She would stay at Bathurst while he went on to another property on the Murrumbidgee River. Their first night was spent at Parramatta at a delightful inn, but she had noted that the system of clearing land by 'the total destruction of every native tree and shrub' left the country so treated 'bare, naked, raw and ugly'.

The next part of the journey was enjoyable and the experience of carriages and horses being ferried across the river at Penrith a good one, but the hazardous jolting over the inhospitable Blue Mountains road was worse than she had expected.

> ... the main portion of the road is bad *beyond an English comprehension; sometimes natural step-like rocks protuding from dust or sand, one, two, three feet above each other, in huge slabs the width of the track and over these* jumpers *as they are pleasantly termed,*

we had to jolt and bump along as best we might. How our springs stood such unwonted exercise is an enigma still.

They passed a tolerable night at a clean little inn, Blind Biddy's, and next day survived the perils of the mountain descent called Soldier's Pinch.

It was a mass of loose stone continually rolling under the horses' feet and so steep as to be very fatiguing to walk down which I preferred doing, not being reconciled to such roads for driving on.

At the Rivulet Inn the next evening—a new building, gilded and bronzed and painted in twenty different colours—they found the servants all drunk. The food was indifferent, though the intoxicated waitress promised 'plenty o' ale and sperrits'. Louisa was to deplore then, and many times later, the habits of drunkenness so universally found. 'Time, money, character, decency, feeling, principle, ambition and honesty—all sacrificed to the demoralising passion for rum.'

On the return journey the Merediths found the inn servants less tipsy, but as to cleanliness, 'the word and meaning seemed equally unknown within though the paint outside was as bright as ever'. Louisa's description of their night at the Rivulet Inn remains as fresh, as pointed and as perfect as when she wrote it:

On our retiring for the night (in company with a dark brown fat candle that smelt almost insufferably ill) to a freshly painted room with very scanty furniture and a most sombre, hide-the-dirt kind of bed, I examined the linen and believe that half a dozen unwashed chimney sweeps occupying the same bed for a fortnight could not have left evidence of a darker hue. The blankets corresponded well in colour but as to exchange those was totally hopeless we dispensed with them and after great difficulties and eloquent grumbling from the rum-inspired landlady, I obtained some coarse cotton sheets the dampness of which was satisfactory, as it proved they had been acquainted with the wash-tub.

Thrusting the other sable and now inodorous coverings into the farthest corner of the room, I washed my hands and had hopes to think of sleep when a loud knocking at the door aroused us—

'Who's there?'

> 'If you please, ma'am, Missus wants them sheets you pulled off your bed for a gentleman as is just come in!'
> With my parasol I poked the things out on the landing, inly congratulating the happy man destined to enjoy such sweet luxury.[3]

In January 1840 the Merediths moved to Homebush, a property on the Parramatta River about 17 kilometres from Sydney. It was dilapidated but tolerably comfortable, on high ground, with a beautiful view over the river. The land had, as usual, been totally cleared except for three splendid Norfolk pines which Louisa enjoyed as much as she did the animal and bird life. She preferred living so far from the town, though heat and dust and the ever-present mosquitoes were still a constant worry. She now had a baby boy, and the detestable mosquitoes with their horrible allies (fleas) besieged in swarms, 'cruelly tormenting my poor child whose chubby face and fair fat arms are covered with mountainous bites, despite all my care'.

A decision to quit New South Wales and settle permanently in Tasmania (still called Van Diemen's Land) had Louisa's full support.

From the first day she felt happy in Tasmania, with its cooler climate, its soft greens and greys and its considerable number of congenial English people. In the temperate climate in Hobarton she felt she had arrived on the right side of the earth again. She liked the 'rosy' children, the sight of 'positively fashionable ladies *walking* about' and then, as later, she delighted in the company of Lady Jane Franklin, wife of the Governor, Sir John. Louisa and Jane were 'two of a kind', cultivated women of intellectual pursuits; Louisa admired the way in which the Franklins tried to cultivate in 'the unambitious multitude' a taste for science, literature and art. She deplored the unmanly attacks made in some of the public papers on Lady Franklin's kindness and ability which, she felt, should at least be met with gratitude and respect.

The Franklins, Louisa wrote in her next journal, were unpopular with pretty Tasmanians who declared they did not wish to be asked to evening parties and then 'stuck in rooms full of pictures and books and shells and stones and other rubbish with nothing to hear but lectures'. What they really desired was military music and military gentlemen as dancing partners.

Charles Meredith's father had his property Cambria in the south, and the journey down the east coast was made in a newly purchased, 'stout colonial-built conveyance, an ingenious variety of the gig species'. The road was even worse than that over the Blue Mountains, with many horror stretches.

> I could not divert my attention for a moment from the misery of the rough jolting nor dared I trust my baby to the maid's arms for fear she might drop him out whilst saving herself from threatened fractures and dislocations.

Down some very steep places (and up again) the two women walked, Louisa carrying the baby. Charles Meredith's brother 'roped himself to the vehicle and walked behind it, trying to exert an extra pull against the slopes'.

Until their own house could be built on their adjacent property, the family lived with Meredith's father at Cambria, shifting to their own place in August 1842. They would spend nine years there, during which time two more sons would be born.

Louisa's second Australian journal, *My Home in Tasmania*, was published in 1852. 'To our Most Gracious and Beloved Queen this simple chronicle of 9 years in one of HM's most remote colonies is dedicated.'[4]

It is a wonderful record of endurance—of floods, fires and every natural catastrophe, of enjoyment, development and achievements. As a settler's wife and mistress of a settler's house, Louisa's comments on her isolated life there provided an observant and entertaining witness to colonial living. Her convict servants were mostly satisfactory and she treated them well.

> During that time we have been served by prisoners of all grades as ploughmen, shipwrights, shearers, labourers, builders, gardeners, carpenters, masons, blacksmiths, shoe makers, house servants, etc. With one or two exceptions they have served us well and as faithfully as we could desire. What more could be said of any farmer's wife here or in England? 5, 10, or 15 years are common

> periods for prisoner servants remaining in the same service before and after conditional pardon. I lately heard of one who stayed 28 years with another master in a situation of great trust. One has been for the last 8 years cook and Major Domo in our own house, as faithfully and incorruptibly honest. At this very time he and another ticket of leave gardener are the only male prisoners in our lonely house (Mr M. being absent for duties elsewhere) and I feel no more, perhaps less, fearful of attack or molestation than I should in the middle of London.

Louisa was much more than the perfect pioneer wife and mother. Impeccable housekeeper, seamstress for the whole family, teacher to three little boys, loving companion to her husband, she wrote and illustrated several nature and educational books for children during her time in Tasmania. The massive volumes are now collectors' items, meticulously illustrated with her own superb colour plates.

In true Victorian style her verses were often didactic and rambling, filled with classical allusions and with rhyme so contrived that, for example, an ode to Queen Titania finishes one line with 'rich regalia', the next with 'daily a' . . .[5]

Charles Meredith was for a while Police Magistrate in Port Sorell and, as a member of Tasmania's first parliament, held office as Colonial Treasurer and Minister for Lands and Works. When they left the property and lived in Hobart, Louisa, who loved theatre, delighted in taking part in Government House theatricals.

Charles died in 1880. As a widow Louisa had found her income greatly reduced owing to bank failures. The granting of a yearly pension of £100 by the Tasmanian Government, 'for distinguished literary services to the colony', was a welcome benison.

In old age Louisa's health was poor. She had chronic sciatica and was blind in one eye, but when she was almost 80 the indomitable dame went to London to oversee publication of her last book. Three years later she died in Collingwood, Melbourne, on 21 October 1895, leaving as her memorial a remarkable collection of published writings and paintings. Included are the two journals, along with *Grandmamma's Verse Book, Waratah Rhymes for Young Australians, Some of My Bush*

Friends in Tasmania, Tasmanian Sketch Book and *Across the Straits* (about a visit to Victoria). There were also two novels, *Phoebe's Mother* and *Nellie, or Seeking Goodly Pearls.*

Mrs Alexander Macleay

THE ELEGANT MISSES MACLEAY

'Poor Papa,' wrote Fanny Macleay, 'poor darling Papa. He works so hard all the time. I wish I could be of more help to him. Papa has, I fear, too much to attend to.'

Fanny (Frances) Macleay was the eldest of the six daughters of Alexander Macleay, Colonial Secretary, who arrived in Sydney with his wife and the girls in January 1826. The youngest, Barbara, was still a schoolgirl. The three sons would follow later. The two youngest boys were at school in England. The eldest, William Sharp Macleay, had recently been appointed to a government position in Cuba after serving as an attaché at the British Embassy in Paris. To this beloved brother Fanny wrote frequently, her letters filled with domestic trivia and often barbed comment on the local scene, with romantic musings about suitors and appalled acceptance of the horrors of colonial living. Her letters are among the treasures of the Mitchell Library in Sydney.[1]

Alexander Macleay was born in the County of Ross in 1767 to an ancient Scots family which had once been very wealthy but had lost fortune through support for the Stuart cause.[2] He went to London and became partner to a wine merchant named William Sharp. He then took a government position as Chief Clerk with the Prisoners of War Society, becoming Secretary in 1806, and later was Secretary of the Transport Board. After the Napoleonic Wars there was intense competition for jobs and many government changes were made. At the age of 50, Macleay found his position abolished.

A pension of £750 per year allowed the family to live in seemingly good circumstances for the next eight years. Macleay was a renowned botanist and entomologist, a Fellow of the Royal and Linnean Societies. Insects were his passion and his collection was regarded as the finest in private hands. He was not, however, as skilled with money management as with plants and insects and in 1825 he was almost forced from retirement to accept appointment as Colonial Secretary to New South Wales at a salary of £2000 per year, with an extra £750 to compensate for the loss of his pension.

There was a large family, although the Macleay children were the survivors of a much larger one. William Sharp was born in 1792, the year after Alexander Macleay and Miss Elizabeth Barclay were married. Infant deaths were a statistic that parents were apparently expected to accept stoically, but if seventeen babies had been born to Mrs Macleay (as one authority records), the survival rate was low even in times when an epidemic might carry off several children within a week.

The girls were all single. They were considered outstandingly attractive, yet none of them seems to have formed an attachment in England. The family's Scots background was impeccable, there were droves of close and distant relatives of high social standing and Papa knew many important people, particularly in the scientific world. Potential husbands there must have been, but the girls' destinies were to be decided on the far side of the world. Perhaps their parents decided they would have splendid chances *out there*—all those younger sons of good families, with lucrative jobs in the colony; all those well-connected officials from powerful English families!

Through their marriages the Macleay girls would indeed be connected to most of the desirable colonial families—and their descendants even more so. Margaret became the wife of Archibald Innes, senior military officer in the Port Macquarie district; Rosa Roberta married Captain Arthur Pooley Onslow and their son married Elizabeth, only daughter of James Macarthur of Camden. Christianne Susan married Colonel Dumaresq, brother-in-law of Governor Darling, and one of their five children later married Louis Hope, 7th Earl of Hopetoun, whose great-nephew became Australia's first Governor-General. When she was 20 Barbara Sibella wed Peter Laurentz Campbell, ADC to Governor Bourke. Fanny was the last to marry, when she was 36, her husband being Thomas Cuthbert Harrington, Assistant Colonial Secretary. Only one of them, Kennethina, never married (although she was said to have refused the hand of Mr Thomas Iceley).

The 'elegant and beautiful Misses Macleay' were received into polite Sydney society immediately. They quite captivated the gentlemen and were soon bright stars on the social scene. Before long they were on very friendly terms with Governor and Mrs Darling, also relative newcomers. Mrs Darling, formerly Elizabeth Dumaresq, seems to have considered Fanny as a suitable wife for her brother, who was the Governor's Private Secretary. Fanny wrote to William:

> Papa is very much pleased with Colonel Dumaresq. He is certainly a very clever and accomplished man but I cannot say I like him. Mrs Darling wishes me to believe that he thinks better of me than I deserve and makes the belief she would be delighted if I were to

> become a connection of hers. Papa believes all this and I really think he is anxious that such an affair should take place but I know myself that the gentleman does not like me any more than I like him. I cannot understand Mrs Darling's behaviour.

Not long after the Macleays' arrival Sir John Jamieson had asked for the hand in marriage of Susan (Christianne Susan). He was very wealthy, had a splendid mansion called Regentville along the Penrith road and was a most influential man whose wife would undoubtedly be one of the first ladies in the colony. Mrs Macleay thought it would be an admirable match, but Susan could not agree. Sir John was not only thirty years her senior, he was gouty and peppery and 'not lovable'. Susan wrote: 'My mother wishes me to sell myself and marry Sir John but my heart fails me'. Wise Susan! Her later marriage was by her own choice and was a happy one. (Many years later, when he was 68, Sir John married his housekeeper, Mary, by whom he already had two sons and five daughters.) Fanny told William that Sir John had asked her first, but she declined as she had no wish to change her name, finding it too pretty. She also wrote:

> I really detest Sir John Jamieson but am obliged to go to-morrow to Regentville. We cannot get off from that, one must comply and the thing is to do it with good grace . . . Papa, Mama, Rosa, Barbara and I set off on this long talked of visit. I hope to return on Thursday when the other three young ladies will take their share of the country.

Fanny was no more complimentary about John Macarthur:

> . . . old King John is of all of them the most disagreeable. He quarrels with everyone who does not give implicit obedience to his opinions and I think the very look of the man would make you shudder. At least it has that effect on me.

Once or twice in letters to her brother Fanny mentions that Colonel Dumaresq had called, but obviously Mrs Darling was mistaken in believing that he was interested in her. It was Susan who married the Colonel, in a big, fashionable wedding in October 1830. They lived for a while on a large property in the upper Hunter River area. Later they moved to Sydney, where their beautiful home Tivoli survives as Kambala, a well-known girls' school.

Fanny had much to tell William about their new life. Of their house, an official residence in Macquarie Place (where Mary Reibey's house had become the Bank of NSW nine years before), Fanny wrote:

> ... it has to be one of the worst and ugliest in Sydney. The Government has ordered some additions to be made which when completed will certainly add much to our comfort.

When the work was in progress she sent detailed drawings to William and added news of robberies in the house by the workmen who, because of carelessness on the part of the servants, had carried off:

> ... 16 tablespoons, 12 large silver forks, 12 dessert spoons, 2 sauce ladles. Papa has offered £40 reward but we heard nothing. I fear we never shall. The lower orders here, if free, are the most impudent, independent creatures you could imagine and as idle as can be.

Fanny, on finance:

> ... a new bank has been set afloat and Papa has very kindly given us each a share in it. They say it will become a profitable concern. You have no idea how exorbitant everything is in this hole, I mean in price, eatables, drinkables, wearables and yet silly people dress themselves in the most extravagant manner and the lower orders squander money away to satisfy any idle fancy.

On romance:

> Your sisters have their heads nearly turned with the flattery that is poured out upon them by the gay youth of this place ... poor Margaret is over head and ears in the tender passion for Archie Innes ...

And on the lack of servants, about which every English lady in the colony complained:

> ... have I mentioned we are in danger of starvation? We cannot find a cook. This is a sad grievance and one we feel very sensibly just

> *now since we ought to have many parties, there being a large number of strangers here and Naval ships in harbour . . .*

The first year in Sydney must have been an exciting one for the sisters, who were all sought after by the gentlemen. Their complaints about the house, their lack of clothes and servants, too many parties ('I sometimes wish we could live in a bark hut where we would not be constantly striving to keep up appearances of respectability') would have been handsomely redressed by the knowledge that they were indeed 'belles'.

> *Young Mr Arthur Onslow, the very charming son of a gay fox-hunting English Parson paid a man a dollar to hang about the house in Macquarie Place and let him know when the Misses Macleay went out.*[3]

To William, Fanny wrote about one of her beaux:

> *. . . who is rather inclined to social success. He was fully intentioned about a fortnight since to sell his property but the ball at Government House had such an effect on his heart and head that he now objects that he cannot think of quitting Sydney. The Misses Macleay are so fascinating and so elegant!! that he cannot go away while they remain. There it is. Promising obviously, as if all the men in the world were seeking our elegant hands!*

Papa was well aware of the charms of his girls, and so determined to see them recognised that once when the regimental band was playing he insisted they must all sally forth to walk about the triangle of grass in front of their house. Almost at once they were joined there by a group of beaux who paraded them to the sound of music until they were all 'quite tired'.

Fanny to William again:

> *I must tell you that your sisters certainly shine here for really the other ladies are, I think, very stupid, ill-tempered or ugly so that we receive all the attention of the gentlemen whom I believe behave politely to us in order to tease the other poor ladies far more than from any approbation of our conduct. I tell my sisters that we shall be treated in the same way presently should there be a fresh importation from England.*

Young Annabella Innes, who frequently visited the house in

Macquarie Place, loved the Macleays and the warmth and hospitality of their home. She used to sit on the floor watching Kennethina ('dear Aunt Kenny') with great interest while her hair was being dressed for a fashionable party.

> Her hair was very red and she was not pretty but I admired her very much. Her hair was dressed in a wonderful erection at the back, supported by a high backed tortoiseshell comb and in front, curls.[4]

The girls may have grumbled about the smallness of their house, but found it large enough to give a ball and supper party for ninety persons. Doors were taken off their hinges, window sashes were removed and the space filled with garlands of flowers. Fanny reported that it was generally said to have been the prettiest thing of the kind ever seen in Sydney. Everyone had been pleased, from the Governor down to the ensigns. Mrs Darling had decided to give a special ball to celebrate the King's birthday and invited some of the sisters to visit her daily to help. 'Papa will be pleased,' Fanny told William, of this easy relationship with Government House. She had cause to complain on another occasion, however, when the Governor's wife started a School of Industry for twenty young 'unfortunate' girls and asked the Macleays to help with sewing layettes and raising money. Fanny became a most unwilling Treasurer-Secretary and assured her brother that the office gave her a great deal of trouble.

Though Fanny would spend the rest of her life in Sydney, she was always critical of the place and looked fondly back towards England. Report of the arrival of an English ship in harbour would send her running to the window in the hope of letters arriving from Home. After one disappointment she wrote:

> ... much patience is required in this place which is a vile nasty hole, possessing nothing capable of gratifying any of our five senses. In short, it is detestable.

On the sense of sight, at least, this was an unfair judgment since the upstairs windows had a fine view of the sea and the constant movements of ships from all parts of the world. The girls spent much leisure time observing the Sydney scene from there and when they found they could actually see some of the officers they knew taking their ease in the parade ground, they were sometimes guilty of watching them through a telescope. They took their sewing upstairs with them, for they made most of their own clothes. Papa was not good with money and it was often a struggle for the elegant Misses Macleay to keep up appearances. They had fewer servants than most people they knew and had to do more domestic work 'than comparable with a neat and ladylike appearance'. When Margaret married Archie Clunes Innes in 1829 her sisters made her complete trousseau. 'When she went on her honeymoon Margaret wore neither bonnet nor gown not made by our poor paws.'

Fanny had, of course, kept her brother William informed of the ups and downs of this romance. 'Margaret and Captain Innes are much attached to each other and would become one soon if they knew how to manage about money matters.' She made gloomy predictions:

> *He has been appointed Commandant to Port Macquarie where he may have about £700 in the course of the ten months he is likely to remain but this would be poor provision for married life. I sometimes think Margaret is more partial to him than he to her. I hope not . . .*

Fanny need not have worried. It was a most successful marriage. The family prospered and their house near Port Macquarie became a great centre of hospitality in the district.[5] The Macleay and Innes families were doubly linked later when younger brother George Macleay married Archie's sister Barbara.

Alexander Macleay was anxious to have a farm. He had received several land grants and had important plans for his 22 hectares at Elizabeth Bay. Meanwhile for his country property he had acquired, by grant and purchase, land near Cobbitty and here Brownlow Hill was established. George Macleay arrived from England in 1827 to take charge of it and was joined by his brother James. Young and adventurous, George later joined Sturt on expeditions to the Murray and Murrumbidgee Rivers, and the Rufus River was named after him for his red hair and beard. Brother James was a greater favourite with Fanny. 'He is satirical and clever but frequently more severe in language than is becoming in so young a man.'

The first house at Brownlow Hill was a small, neat building seated on a gentle hill overlooking a field of ripe wheat. By 1834 William was informed that 'it has been extended and improved and is now pronounced one of the best in the colony'. It is there still.[6]

Macleay's great achievement, however, was Elizabeth Bay House, a white mansion standing in acres of lawns and gardens that ran down to the harbour.[7] It was rumoured that up to £7000 had been spent on the grounds alone. 'It is one of the most perfect places I ever saw,' one observer wrote.

The white Palladian mansion was designed by John Verge, the outstanding architect of the day. It was a grand house built around a central, domed salon. The staircase curved up to a circular gallery around which were bedrooms and sitting rooms. Macleay and Verge put their magnificent visions into being and in 1839 Mr and Mrs Macleay and their two unmarried children, Kennethina and William Sharp, moved in to Elizabeth Bay House.

Macleay had overreached himself, however, in the building and magnificent furnishings of his mansion. Much of it had to go in 1845 when, heavily in debt, he sold the drawing-room furniture (twelve chairs and matching sofas of Brazilian rosewood, covered with yellow silk tabaret with touches of crimson and yellow silk cord) to be used for the new Government House. In the early 1840s he had to sell some of his land and, after making over the house and its remaining contents to his son William, to whom he was in debt, he, his wife and Kennethina moved out to live at Tivoli with Susan and her family.

By a fluke of history, Elizabeth Bay House is still standing. Members of the family lived there until 1903, after which it endured many subtractions, alterations and other indignities. The grounds shrank, to the extent that the house now opens straight on to a street and blocks of high-rise flats crowd around it, but the views out across the harbour are still superb. Rooms and walls were altered and in 1941 it was converted into flats, but the wonderful staircase seems to have been the pivot to hold it for posterity. In 1972 plans were made to restore Elizabeth Bay House and it is now open to the public and administered by a trust.

Fanny did not live to see the house completed, but she wrote happily of a gay party in the garden with 150 persons to 'déjeuner in a sylvan bower' in 1836. That was the year of her marriage to Thomas Harrington, of whom she had earlier written:

> ... *this person is much admired by my sisters but I am much afraid of him for he is very clever and, I think, satirical so that I avoid his company.*

Later she wrote to William of her admiration for her 'husband to be'.

They were married on 26 June, spent their honeymoon at Brownlow Hill and returned to Sydney. Fanny died two months after her wedding. Alexander Macleay, whose constant companion she had been, was devastated.

'Poor darling Papa', who worked so hard all the time, continued to do so. He was elected a Member of Parliament when he was 78, having opened his campaign from Lake Innes House, the home of his daughter Margaret. Later he became the first Speaker of the Legislative Council. He died in 1848 as a result of being thrown out of his carriage while on the way to visit Government House.

It was then twenty-two years since the Macleay girls had taken Sydney by storm. Susan and Kennethina would have had wonderful memories of their days of beaux and belles and balls, of their 'poor paws' stitching away to renovate gowns and bonnets, of cheerful Fanny, always filled with gossip, always writing those long, long letters to William . . .

Annabella Boswell

A PASSIONATE AUSTRALIAN — ANNABELLA BOSWELL

In 1916 an old lady died, in Scotland. She was not famous, though many years earlier she had enjoyed modest literary success with the publication of several small books of recollections and observations gleaned from early life in Australia.[1] The books had sharply illuminated living conditions and social customs in that distant land where the very lively old lady, Mrs Annabella Boswell, had been born. They were not about the conditions or customs of convicts or emancipists, however, but of the Australian gentry, for Mrs Boswell had been Annabella Alexandrina Campbell Innes, very well connected with good

Scots families both through her own parents and her husband's. Her birth, on a property near Bathurst in September 1826, might never have happened had not her grandfather Campbell of Bredalbane been a close friend of the Governor, Major Lachlan Macquarie, who had suggested that the Campbells might emigrate with some of their eight sons and five daughters. The Innes side of the family was equally prolific, for grandmother Innes had produced six daughters and ten sons.[2] Two of the older boys died in battle and the two youngest girls were named for them—Gordina and Williamina. Both later became names for new generations.

George Innes, Annabella's father, was the eighth son of Major James Innes of Thrumster, Caithness, and Margaret Clunes. When George sailed for Sydney in 1823 his brother, Archibald Clunes Innes of the 3rd Buffs, was Captain of the Guard of soldiers in charge of the convicts. George Innes, relating family stories to his daughter Annabella later on, remembered that his father had been sent a blank army commission in 1815 and had decided that the sixth son, Archie, still a schoolboy, should accept it. The boy was brought home, encased in uniform and taken to London. Just before his fifteenth birthday he was on his way to Belgium to join Wellington's army. It was Archie who married Miss Margaret Macleay, daughter of the Colonial Secretary, in October 1829.

George Innes took up a land grant in the Bathurst district. There he built a cottage, a mill and a cattle outstation which he called Umbiella. In October 1825, at the age of 23, he married 20-year-old Margaret Campbell. Annabella was born the next year, her sister Margaret almost three years later.[3]

Country living suited both children, who delighted in the freedom of the bush. They were allowed to play with the little black girl Maria, the only child in the much-diminished local Capita tribe, and took pleasure in telling her stories about Queen Victoria, in what they called 'broken English'. To the tribe, Annabella wrote later, Queen Victoria was a very great lady indeed as she possessed an unlimited supply of blankets. To commemorate her birthday all the Aborigines could apply at the nearest government store and get a new blanket; as this happened at the beginning of winter, it seemed to them to be a particularly good way for a great lady to celebrate such an important day.

Annabella was a bright little girl who learned to read and write very early and began to keep a journal when she was very young. She rarely came in contact with the seamier side of life, in spite of living in the bush and the fact that all the servants were convicts. Until the *Red Rover* arrived in Sydney in September 1832 with 202 women immigrants on board, the Innes family had been well satisfied with their servants.

> We had at this time a very nice servant who had been my sister's nurse and our cook was a clever Irishwoman, Kitty Coner by name, the wife of an old soldier who was constable, under my father, a district magistrate. Ann, our favourite, was going to marry our shoemaker, a very decent man; both were English and both also were convicts.

After Ann's marriage the family asked for two new servants from the *Red Rover*. The new arrivals were an unpleasant surprise. The women on this ship were notorious for their loose conduct and gave rise to the term 'she's a Red Rover' as a byword for immorality. They did not last long in the Innes household. 'Such *creatures* they turned out to be!'

Annabella had been given regular lessons by her mother, but when she was 8 it was decided to send her to school in Sydney.

> . . . early in 1834 I found myself settled at school in Bridge Street, under the care of Mrs Evans and her friend and partner Miss Ferris. Mr Evans had a large bookseller's and stationer's shop and we occupied the rest of the house. It faced the old Government Stores and close by flowed the Tank Stream, now arched over and made into the main drain of that portion of the populous city.

The school was close to old Government House and to Macquarie Place, where the leading government officials all lived in two-storey houses with pretty gardens, set well back from the street. There Annabella often visited Mr and Mrs Macleay, 'our family's kind friends', and became very fond of the remaining 'elegant and beautiful Misses Macleay'. She was told years later that Fanny Macleay had expressed a wish to adopt and educate her. 'And I loved very much dear Aunt Kenny'.

Annabella stayed with the Macleays after a flood caused the Tank Stream to overflow and inundate houses, including the schoolhouse basement. The girls were evacuated when a party of soldiers went to the rescue. Annabella was sure that the rescue was great fun both for the young officers and for the older students who were carried to safety in strong male arms. Such a miserable little urchin as herself, she felt, could not have provided much pleasure!

While she was with the Macleays she met Mrs Sturt, whose husband Captain Charles Sturt was then away with an exploring party near the Murrumbidgee River. She also went driving with Mr Macleay to inspect the mansion being built for him at Elizabeth Bay. She loved to play in the vast garden ('one of the loveliest situations in the Colony') while adults were busy discussing plans for the house.

Her school was relocated at Miller's Point, but Annabella, always homesick, did not remain there long. She was delighted when, after a year, her father arrived to take her back home for good, making the journey in his new gig. They now had a new home in the same district, called Glen Alice, where the girls enjoyed helping their mother plan and lay out a garden. They took native plants from their favourite picnic place near the creek, and begged cuttings from friends.

A governess, Miss Willis, became part of the family's station life and Annabella's zest for learning was encouraged. The child 'panted for information', learned the histories of England, Scotland, Greece and Rome and read every book in the house (except Shakespeare which, she was disappointed to discover, her mother found unsuitable). The invaluable Miss Willis, who had a passion for grammar and kept the girls hard at their learning, also taught Annabella the guitar. Another skill Annabella learned as a child was to crack a stockwhip, an accomplishment which later amazed several gentlemen at Lake Innes House displaying their own talents with the whip.

Station owners did a great deal of visiting, on a scale and of a duration that could never happen now, made possible then only by the availability of convict and ex-convict labour. A visiting family would arrive like a general caravanserai — horses, grooms, gig, luggage, cart, babies, nursemaids, governesses and other servants. The Innes family spent three months with their close friends and relatives the Rankens, also station people with eight children of their own; three months with other friends; and later, mother and the girls would live for years at Port Macquarie with Major and Mrs Innes.

George Innes, advised by a doctor in Sydney that his poor health needed a warmer climate, went with his family to stay as the guests of his brother Archie at Port Macquarie. It was then a long and difficult journey because the road across the Blue Mountains was rough, hilly, stony and extremely hazardous. They set off in March 1839. The girls found this first part of the journey a great adventure. A dray was sent ahead, loaded with a tent and provisions for the two nights they would spend in the bush before reaching a place, only 32 kilometres distant, where a carriage and horses would take them on to Sydney in greater comfort and speed.

They travelled in what Annabella called 'a carriage and five', a large dray piled with mattresses and pillows and drawn by five strong bullocks. The girls and their governess rode in the dray, the parents followed in the gig and a friend and the groom rode alongside. After 15 kilometres they camped at Coco Creek, where the tent was pitched in a wild but sheltered spot.

> *Two bright fires had been kindled. The horses were tethered to the trees or set loose with hobbles on. A carpet was soon spread under the tent and two trunks set up as tables near the entrance. On them we spread a snowy cloth and began with eager hands to arrange the good things that had been so liberally provided. We had taken everything we could think of to make us comfortable. The little brass kettle was soon handed up with tea, a basin of sugar and a bottle of milk, while wine was drawn for those who preferred it. The first evening all our provisions were cold but a coop with some plump chickens in it promised that if we should be detained longer than we expected we need not starve. The weather was still too hot for us to carry with us any uncooked supplies.*

It took a long time for the cumbersome transport to get out of the valley, with a great deal of up-and-downing, dismounting and scrambling about. When they reached the Water

Holes, where there was a chain of lagoons and an unattractive accommodation house, the family decided to camp out. It was a general meeting place and many drays were there, taking bales of wool to Sydney or bringing supplies back, women and children sometimes perched high on top of the loaded drays. The primitive inn had a poor reputation for comfort, being infested with 'creatures'. One unfortunate woman was said to have lain awake all night ringing a small handbell continuously in an effort to keep the bugs away. Another traveller declared they had actually dragged him from bed!

They arrived at Port Macquarie in mid-April and were met by Major Innes and his wife. The Macleay girls, who had often wondered whether he would ever be able to afford to marry their sister Margaret, need not have worried. Archibald Innes had become a rich and important man, the senior military officer in the district, living in great style in an oasis cleared from the bush about 11 kilometres from the little township. Lake Innes House was large, extremely comfortable and beautifully furnished. Furniture in the large drawing-room was upholstered in yellow satin damask, there were family portraits in the library and on one wall a painting by Veronese.

The place was self-sufficient with its kitchen gardens, orchards, vines and stables, and the family and its many guests were looked after by a large staff of convict servants. In the grounds was Bachelors Hall, three bedrooms and a sitting room, where any of the young military men or graziers of the district could spend the night and appear at mealtimes in the big house. There were sometimes eighteen to breakfast. From his large stable Major Innes made horses available to any of the new young officers, a handsome gesture which was much appreciated.

There were two girl cousins, Dido and Gordina, and a small boy, Gustavus. Major Innes's sister Barbara lived with them and later doubled the family connection by marrying George Macleay.

They stayed for seven months. George's health had improved so much that they planned to return home in September, but he became suddenly worse and died, aged 37, on 17 August. Mother and daughters finally made the long, troublesome trip back to the Bathurst property in November. Mrs Innes was a capable station manager, growing wheat, looking after cattle and making cheese and butter, some for sale on the Sydney market. The house had some fine cedar furniture, made on the property from local wood by their own carpenter and a cabinet maker from Sydney. The girls did daily lessons for the next two years, but enjoyed the freedom and stimulation of station life and loved the fact that they were able to run wild, like their favourite river.

They moved to Parramatta for a while, then in January 1843 returned to Port Macquarie. They intended to rent a cottage in the town, but Major Innes's insistent hospitality kept them at Lake Innes House for eight years. These years stayed in Annabella's mind for ever, and the old lady who wrote her recollections saw her time there as 'clothed in sunshine and decked with flowers', filled with the smell of the bush and the sounds of birds and the sea.

> *Australian in heart as well as by birth, my mind often wanders from present scenes and memory is busy with the primitive surroundings of my early life, the happy years of my childhood and the still happier years which followed.*

In 1843 Cousin Dido was now almost 11, Gordina nearly 8, and Gustavus five. There was a new little boy called St Clair, and two other babies had died. Annabella and Margaret were older, but the cousins were always very close and Major Innes was delighted to have his 'four girls' always about the house and the company of his sister-in-law to replace the loved sister who had married George Macleay.

Annabella was now 16 and, at 1·74 metres, considered to be a very tall girl. She very much enjoyed the social life at Lake Innes House, which seemed to be a centre for district activities. People rode in from their stations to spend a few days or to await arrival or departure of the steamer, which was due in on Saturday morning and left on Monday if the tide and the sandbar permitted. She was interested in gardening and flower arranging, loved riding and swimming and, with mother and aunt very open-minded on female activities, the party from Lake Innes often enjoyed sea bathing.

In 1843 the booming economy in the colony had flattened somewhat and the lifestyle at Lakes Innes was less grand than before, but to Annabella everything seemed very luxurious.

> We were told that nearly all the servants had been dismissed but there was still a butler and two footmen, a piper who assisted when wanted and two Spaniards who were attached to the stables but appeared in the house in livery at times. They looked very smart and waited well. My aunt had a maid and my cousins had a nice Highland maid who came to the colony in the same ship with our maid Christina and afterwards married the piper. There were also two housemaids and a laundress. All the years we were at the Lake my aunt and we four girls all wore white dresses, which entailed a good deal of work but if the climate made it almost necessary it also favoured the laundress. We wore alpaca or fine merino in winter, changing invariably on the 14th of May and 15th October.

Bruce, the piper, was a most important person in this traditional Scots household. Long verandahs flanked three sides of the house and when there were large dinner parties or several guests staying, in the early morning and evening the bush silence was broken by the skirl of the bagpipes as the kilted Bruce marched along the verandahs.

During the visit of Alexander Macleay (the former Colonial Secretary and Margaret Innes's father) there were parties and there was piping almost continuously. Aged 78, Macleay was seeking election to the first Legislative Assembly and began his election campaign from Lake Innes. The bagpipes sounded every evening as the lively old gentleman led the group in vigorous Scots and country dancing. Annabella was now old enough to dine with the guests and, at one grand dinner during this time,

> I felt quite dazzled. I had never seen so splendid an entertainment. The table presented a magnificent appearance, handsomely laid for 18 persons. The epergne with flowers (which I had arranged) was in the centre of the table and as high as the lamp. With it were two silver wine coolers with light wines and branch candlesticks with wax candles and four silver side dishes; we had two soups and an immense variety of dishes. Bruce and the butler waited and we had four footmen in livery.
>
> The ladies had all been busy making pink election favours and

gathered at the gate to see the gentlemen depart, watched by an admiring crowd of Aborigines profusely decorated with pink calico. Six horsemen bearing flags rode before the procession all the way.[4]

Macleay was elected for Port Macquarie and became the first Speaker of the Legislative Council.

The truly great event of the Port Macquarie years was the visit early in 1847 of the Governor, Sir Charles Fitzroy, and Lady Mary. Windows were polished, rooms were turned out and the girls were as busy with preparations for the vice-regal visit as were the servants. 'His Excellency,' wrote Annabella,

> is immensely tall and stout; Lady Mary is also very tall and stout and has but slight remains of the good looks for which she was remarked in her youth in Ireland with her father, the Duke of Richmond.

Mr Charles Fitzroy, 'tall and slight and immensely good looking, is his father's secretary'.

There was dancing every night and during the day Lady Mary, a most industrious committee lady, kept them all busy making things for the Sydney School of Industry bazaar. 'Such knitting, crocheting and work of every kind was never seen!'

The girls were introduced to the polka, 'a new dance and not to know it argues you yourself unknown'. Dr and Mrs Dawson were with the official party and Mrs Dawson offered to teach this new dance . . . 'she is a little woman, all full skirts and stiff petticoats. This too is a new fashion and our visitors are rather shocked at our primitive style of dress'.

However, they sent to Sydney for stiff muslin for petticoats, and Lady Mary sent for her polka music. They were soon 'polking' expertly, the girls rendered more fashionable by the addition of stiff petticoats. The Governor himself complimented them on having made good the deficiency. Annabella had been told that fashionable ladies could never wear too many petticoats and that a lady should be able to see her bustle when she looked back over her shoulder!

When the Governor and his party left to visit New England, Annabella was honoured by being allowed to tie on his fly-veil of blue purse silk that one of the ladies had netted. Mr Charles Fitzroy wore a green veil wrapped around a tall white hat, which amused Miss Innes so much she made a rhyme about it: 'contrived a double debt to pay;/curtains by night, to save his eyes by day'. With his curtained hat Mr Fitzroy wore long boots with a great piece cut out under the knee, dark-coloured 'unutterables' (trousers), a stable jacket and waistcoat of small black and white check, a coloured shirt and neckerchief. It was a smart bushman's costume for 1847.

The girls later attended a ball at Government House in Sydney and, at a dinner given by Mrs Dawson, Annabella went in on the arm of Captain William Blyth O'Connell, grandson of Governor Bligh. She celebrated her 21st birthday with a beach picnic at Port Macquarie. Six weeks later they were all saddened and depressed by news of the death of Lady Mary, killed when the horses bolted and her carriage overturned soon after leaving Government House at Parramatta to spend Christmas in Sydney.

The great days of Lake Innes House were over by 1850. Major Innes could no longer afford such lavish entertainments; the 1840s depression had taken its toll, and cheap labour supplies dried up with the end of transportation. He became Police Magistrate in Newcastle and died there in 1857. After a succession of occupants, the great house began to crumble and the bush to take over. It was finally destroyed in a bushfire.

Annabella also lived in Newcastle for some years after she married, aged almost thirty. Patrick Charles Douglas-Boswell was a Scot with a distinguished family background. He had come to Australia to settle on the land, but later became a teller with the Bank of New South Wales and in 1858 was manager of the Newcastle branch. He and Annabella were married in Newcastle on 17 June 1856. Eight years later they visited England and Scotland, and settled in Scotland after he inherited family property there.

Annabella never returned to Australia, although she thought about the country and her enjoyable life there more and more. She told her children many stories of 'colonial life', published several books of 'recollections' and 'gleanings' and remained always, at heart, a passionate Australian.

*Elizabeth Anne Tripp,
immigrant from Somerset, 1850s*

A FIVE-POUND FUTURE

In the years after the Napoleonic Wars a great depression of mind and spirit, brought about by empty pockets, unemployment and a future obscured by the blackest of clouds, spread through the British Isles. Poverty was an activator which would take many thousands of emigrants looking for a better life to the other side of the world. People were starving in the towns and barely existing in the countryside. Single men in cities sometimes worked for 3 or 4 shillings a week rather than go to a workhouse; a farm labourer with a wife and five or six children might receive a weekly wage of 8 shillings.

For the single woman life was truly bleak. There was an enormous excess of women over men and there were too few jobs and too many applicants. Yet in the colony there was almost as great an excess of males. Not only had many more male convicts been transported, but voluntary migrants had been mainly masculine, fitting exactly the strong belief of man as superior being; 'man's love of adventuring, self-reliance, indifference to family ties all being qualities which lead to a desire for male expatriation'.

With such an imbalance it was obviously highly desirable to get women out of Britain and into the colony. In 1831 the British Government began its first assisted migration scheme and soon started a special one for women. In March 1834 The Committee for Female Emigration to Australia was placing posters in shops and offices all over the country, advising of the impending departure of the vessel *David Scott*.[1]

In search of a five-pound future, in search of a husband in many cases, looking for a new way of life which could only be better than the old (for it could scarcely be worse), women went on board, one wave in the tide of female emigration which flowed into Australia in the 1830s, 1840s and 1850s.

The footnote of the poster testified to a happy result for the young women who had already emigrated on the *Bussorah Merchant*.[2] An advertisement for that voyage had appeared the year before, a notice to 'Young Women Desirous of Bettering Their Condition By An EMIGRATION TO NEW SOUTH WALES'. Under an experienced and respectable man and wife engaged as superintendents, unmarried women and widows of good health and character were invited to apply to the committee in London. The opening paragraph had been tempting:

> *In New South Wales and Van Diemen's Land there are very few Women compared with the whole number of People, so that it is impossible to get Women enough as Female Servants or for other Female Employment. The consequence is, that desirable situations, with good wages, are easily obtained by Females in these Countries; but the Passage is so long that few people can pay the expence [sic] of it without help. There is now, however, the following favourable opportunity of going to New South Wales.*

Female Emigration TO AUSTRALIA.

COMMITTEE:

EDWARD FORSTER, Esq. *Chairman*
SAMUEL HOARE, Esq.
JOHN TAYLOR, Esq.
THOMAS LEWIN, Esq.
S. H. STERRY, Esq.

CHARLES HOLTE BRACEBRIDGE, Esq.
JOHN S. REYNOLDS, Esq.
JOHN PIRIE, Esq.
CAPEL CURE, Esq.
WILLIAM CRAWFORD, Esq.

CHARLES LUSHINGTON, Esq.
JOHN ABEL SMITH, Esq. M.P.
GEORGE LONG, Esq.
COLONEL PHIPPS,
NADIR BAXTER, Esq.
CAPTAIN DANIEL PRING, R.N.

The Committee for promoting the Emigration OF Single Women

To AUSTRALIA, acting under the Sanction of His Majesty's Secretary of State for the Colonies, HEREBY GIVE NOTICE, That

THE SPLENDID TEAK-BUILT SHIP

"David Scott," of 773 Tons Register,

Carrying an experienced Surgeon, and a respectable Person and his Wife as Superintendents to secure the Comfort and Protection of the Emigrants during the Voyage will sail from

GRAVESEND
On Thursday 10th of July next,

(Beyond which day she will on no account be detained) direct for

SYDNEY.

Single Women and Widows of good Character, from 15 to 30 Years of Age, desirous of bettering their Condition by Emigrating to that healthy and highly prosperous Colony, where the number of Females compared with the entire Population is greatly deficient, and where consequently from the great demand for Servants, and other Female Employments, the Wages are comparatively high, may obtain a Passage

On payment of FIVE POUNDS only.

Those who are unable to raise even that Sum here, may, when approved by the Committee, go *without any Money Payment whatever*, as their Notes of Hand will be taken, payable in the Colony within a reasonable time after their arrival, when they have acquired the means to do so: in both cases the Parties will have the advantage of the **Government Grant** in aid of their Passage.

The Females who proceed by this Conveyance will be taken care of on their first Landing at Sydney. They will find there a List of the various Situations to be obtained, and of the Wages offered, and will be perfectly free to make their own Election; they will not be bound to any person, or subjected to any restraint, but will be, to all intents and purposes, perfectly free to act and decide for themselves.

Females in the Country, who may desire to avail themselves of the important advantages thus offered them, should apply by Letter to "The Emigration Committee, London," under Cover addressed to "The UNDER SECRETARY OF STATE, COLONIAL DEPARTMENT, LONDON." It will be necessary that the Application be accompanied by a Certificate of Character from the Resident Minister of the Parish, or from some other respectable persons to whom the Applicant may be known; but the Certificate of the Resident Minister is in all cases most desirable. Such Females as may find it expedient may, when approved by the Committee as fit persons to go by the Conveyance, be boarded temporarily in London, prior to Embarkation, on Payment of 7s. per Week.

All Applications made under cover in the foregoing manner, or personally, will receive early Answers, and all necessary Information, by applying to

JOHN MARSHALL, Agent to the Committee, 26, Birchin Lane, Cornhill, London
EDWARD FORSTER, *Chairman*

NOTE.—The Committee have the satisfaction to state that of 217 Females who went out by the "Bussorah Merchant," 180 obtained good Situations within three Days of their Landing, and the remainder were all well placed within a few Days, under the advice of a Ladies' Committee, formed in the Colony expressly to aid the Females on their arrival.

LONDON, 1st May, 1834.

By Authority:
PRINTED BY JOSEPH HARTNELL, FLEET STREET, FOR HIS MAJESTY'S STATIONERY OFFICE.

The same kind of success did not always follow with later ships, and the term 'respectable' was often widely stretched by the shipping agents in London after free immigration was introduced in 1835 and was then followed by the bounty system. Colonists who wanted to sponsor migrants as employees were given a bounty order worth £30 for each married couple under 30 years of age, £15 for a single woman between 15 and 30, £10 for a single man between 18 and 25 and £5 for each child. At such a distance this was a chancy business, and bounty permits were transferred to shipping agents.

Large sums of money could be involved and human greed was not proof against this. Unscrupulous agents often looked the other way at obvious forgeries of character certificates—or even provided them. They did not properly supervise accommodation and food supplies, and allowed emigrants to be exploited after landing.

Not all the women who landed in Australian ports were of the high character expected. Many had come from workhouses and orphanages; some were straight off the streets. 'We have enough loose women in Sydney without the further benefit of London's street sweepings,' one colonist complained. In another instance, two women, Mary Ann Barnes of Lambeth, 'an incorrigible drunkard and prostitute', and Elizabeth Mathews, ditto, were immediately recognised on the wharf by soldiers of the 17th Regiment who had been stationed at Chatham where the women had worked the streets.[3]

With fevers, deaths and frequent fires, conditions on some of the ships were almost as bad as they had been on convict ships. Many of them *were* converted convict ships. There were high profits to be made and there was no real health supervision. Nor was there insistence on adequate sanitary provision on board. The convict ship *John Barry*, which had one bathtub and two privies when it carried 300 convicts, was 'converted' for emigration and carried 400 people with no extra facilities. The *Lady McNaughton*, which had carried 300 convicts, packed in 400 migrants when it sailed from Ireland in 1836; of these, 185 women were put into quarters with 106 berths and six 'hospital' beds. Some had children with them. The women were ordered below at 5 p.m. each afternoon and could not come up until 8 a.m. next morning. Deck space and passages were crammed with cargo being taken out for sale by the captain. Because of fire risk no lamps were allowed below and on this ship water was rationed. When she sailed into Sydney Harbour the ship flew a distress signal. There had been typhus on board; fifty migrants and seamen had died of it, and fifty-six children died of measles and whooping cough.

Human life when it was poor was not highly respected by officialdom, but this terrible occurrence brought action. Bounty order payments were not to be made until safe arrival in Australia. Statistics on child deaths were also alarming and brought about a further tightening of the laws.

Knavish captains, surgeons with few qualifications (two teaspoons of castor oil every hour was regarded as effective against cholera!), and rotten, leaky, insanitary, crowded ships caused the death of many women emigrants, but thousands kept arriving to help redress the imbalance of the sexes. In 1828 there had been 333 men to every 100 women in the colony. By 1841 the proportion was down to 187 men to every hundred.

The well-publicised *David Scott*, which brought out so many women looking for a five-pound future, had been reasonably well converted, with new strong bulkheads built to separate the women's dormitories from the seamen's quarters. A hundred berths accommodated three or four women each, sleeping side by side like rows of nice little female sardines. One of the bunks was occupied by a farmer's widow and her three daughters; four tall, black-eyed orphaned sisters from Suffolk had another. Citizens of Sydney greeted the ship happily and a *Sydney Morning Herald* journalist wrote a paean to the four sisters: 'if the bachelors of Sydney do not immediately lay siege to their hearts, they must be insensible to beauty and the blandishments of the softer sex'. A Sydney merchant had been equally lyrical about the 217 unmarried females on the *Bussorah Merchant*:

> ... who knows but from these free women or their descendants we shall have some of the future senators of Australia. You would be astonished with what avidity the respectable colonists sought the

services of these young women. The scene was really most interesting, more like a country fair than anything else.⁴

The *Red Rover* and the *Princess Royal*, later ships whose women came mostly from the London Female Penitentiary and the Guardian Asylum, had (and deserved) a different reception, creating local scandals which made life doubly difficult for respectable girls following them. To call a woman a 'Red Rover' or a 'Princess Royal' established her bad reputation at once. The *Princess Royal* had docked in Hobart, where a ladies' committee had rented a house near the waterfront for temporary accommodation. After this, local ladies were not anxious to associate themselves with women emigrants and men frequently behaved atrociously. The arrival of the migrant ship *Strathfieldsaye* in Hobart with 286 women, most of excellent character, was such an occasion. An observer wrote that there were about 2000 men waiting on the jetty and

> . . . as soon as the first boat reached the shore there was a regular rush towards the spot and the half dozen constables present could scarcely open a passage sufficient to allow the females to pass. And now, the most unheard of, disgusting scenes ensued . . . as each female passed on she was jeered by the blackguards and the most vile and brutal language was addressed to every woman. Some brutes even took still further insulting liberties and stopped the women by force, addressed them, pointedly, in the most obscene manner. Any woman with one spark of the feeling of modesty, must have felt this degradation of the most terrible kind and by far the greater portion could bear the insults no longer — scarcely one woman was there but wept, and that bitterly. One poor creature was so overcome she absolutely fainted.⁵

For the women who landed in Adelaide there was accommodation at the Servants' Home. They were met at the docks by the Matron, who was supposed to feed and shelter them for 1 shilling per day until they found work. The supervision was poor, the food the same; when there were no jobs to be found, many of the women took to the streets for a living.⁶

In Melbourne a hotchpotch of wooden buildings in St Kilda Road was used to house emigrants. In 1852 a female barracks was opened in an old army building at the corner of Spencer and La Trobe Streets. Conditions were basic, for the women were to be encouraged to move out as soon as possible. No fires were allowed, lights-out was at 8 p.m., there were cold baths and six patent 'self-acting earth closets' for up to 200 women.

The lack of official care for the welfare of women emigrants after arrival—the failure to make adequate provision for them until they could find work—was not particularly colonial, merely part of the general laissez-faire attitude towards the poor and towards women and children. In England children as young as 6 years old, girls as well as boys, worked underground in coalmines; 9-year-olds spent fifteen-hour days at the looms; and women stripped to the waist were coal-haulers in the mines.

As in other towns, the original ladies' committee had faded away in Sydney. Within weeks of arrival many girls were destitute, and saw prostitution as the solution. Caroline Chisholm[7], almost single-handed at first, stubborn, strong and utterly convinced of the desperate need for succour, helped to reshape the country's future by her vision of these women as wives and mothers, and worked to change the public's attitude towards them.

Caroline had been in Sydney for two years, having remained there while her soldier husband returned to India. She had, while in India, conducted a school for the daughters of soldiers and she itched to do something for girls she knew were sleeping in sheds and fainting from lack of food because no real thought had been given to them after they came off the ships. The years of prosperity were almost ended and employment was now hard to find. Caroline knew she must get the girls away from the towns and into the country, where she was sure there would be work for them.

In a religiously intolerant town, Caroline was a devout Catholic. In an age when ladies did not have opinions, walk unattended in the streets or write letters about social evils to newspapers, she did all three and did them successfully, weathering public opinion as an interferer and busybody. She demanded action of the Governor, Sir George Gipps, in a personal confrontation and, on condition of incurring no government expense, was allowed part of the wooden Immigration Barracks in Bent Street, where a 4·27 metre square storeroom was cleared for her.

The three Chisholm children were left at Windsor with the housekeeper and nurse so that Caroline could move to Sydney. Her first night was fearsome.

> *I retired, weary, to rest. Scarce was the light out, when I fancied from the noise that dogs must be in the room and in some terror I got a light. What I experienced at seeing rats in all directions I cannot describe. My first act was to throw on a cloak and get at the door with the intent of leaving. My second thoughts were, if I did so, my desertion would cause much amusement and ruin my plan. I therefore lighted a second candle and seating myself on my bed, wept there until three rats descending from the roof alighted on my shoulders.*

This proved to be the challenge she needed.

> *I got up with some resolution. I had two loaves and some butter (for my office, bedroom and pantry were one) and I cut the bread into slices, placed the whole in the middle of the room, put a dish of water convenient and with a light by my side I kept my seat on the bed reading* Abercrombie *and watching the rats until four in the morning. I at one time counted thirteen and never less than seven at the dish during the entire night. The following night I gave them a similar treat, with the addition of arsenic and, in this manner passed my first four nights at the home.*

She defeated the rats. Defeating all kinds of opposition was relatively easy for a woman with such stamina, who turned herself into a one-woman employment agency with fantastic success. Her work and her powerful public image caused many other respectable ladies, in both Australia and England, to take an interest in women and the colonies. In England many noble names, including two marquesses and three earls, were on a committee which formed the Fund for Promoting Female Emigration in the winter of 1849. It raised £22 000. 'Some small additions have occasionally been received and a few of the Emigrants have, through their friends, defrayed some portion of the costs of the passage.' After two years the Society felt that

> *. . . the fearful destitution which prevailed in London at the time*

when the society was first established has, no doubt, by a variety of circumstances, been greatly alleviated. Much suffering, however, still prevails, especially in the female portion of the community.

There was still an excess of women over men in England. The 1841 census put it at 320 000; in two years it had become 545 762 and was 'the cause of much suffering and also of immorality'. Between 1850 and 1852 the Society sent out 1071 women to Melbourne, Adelaide, Geelong, Sydney, Hobart, Swan River and Moreton Bay. Its report said:

> Emigration has been universally successful although in some cases, in spite of all precautions, the committee has been deceived as to the character of the migrant and much turbulence has been complained of through the passage. The demand for family servants is on the increase.

This last is borne out in a letter from Messrs J. B. Were of Melbourne (in a different kind of business then than today), written on 7 September 1852:

> The migrants sent out in the Fortitude and the Roxburgh Castle have had our full attention and we are happy to say were provided with good situations immediately on arrival of the ship and turned out very superior. They were immediately hired by respectable families at high rates of wages. We are still in great want of servants for general work and if you can send us 50 women out by every ship, strong in morale and physically, it would be the greatest boon to this country.[8]

What kind of women were they? The shipping lists show lace transferrers (nine), milliners, print and map colourer, shawl and parasol fringer, straw-bonnet makers (eighteen), collar stitchers (three), charwomen, infant's nurse, waterproof coat-maker. Dressmakers were in large supply.

A housemaid who had worked in England for 3 shillings a week went to Mr Grigor of Melbourne at £20 per annum; a hairworker went to J. P. Fawkner, Esq. of Pascoe Vale at £20 per annum; a servant from 1s 6d per week to Mrs J. W. Bell of Collins Street at £25; a servant out of a place and ill for four months to Mr Sayers of La Trobe street at £20; a laundry maid from 6 shillings a week to Mrs Nicholson of St Kilda at £25 per annum.

Lady Jane Franklin

LADY JANE—AN INDEPENDENT SPIRIT

'A woman in trowsers' was one of the unkind things said of her in Hobart Town; 'the power behind the scenes', wrote a newspaper which also accused her of meddling in politics and of trying to influence the Governor, Sir John Franklin, in too many ways. Because she stayed in her room a good deal and did not 'exhibit her fancywork', she was thought to be writing a book and possibly planning some kind of civil revolution.

She was a good-looking woman and dressed well, but not many of Hobart's gentlemen found her attractive because she was so obviously their intellectual superior. Nor was she popular with the ladies, for she tried to *educate* them. She found their conversation trivial and their way of life frivolous and tried to change both by arranging evenings of music, art and lectures at Government House. Hopeful of delightful entertainment waltzing in the arms of handsome, red-coated officers and gentlemen, the ladies found themselves subjected instead to 'improving' programs.

Often it must have seemed to Lady Jane Franklin[1] that she could do nothing right. She had been a great beauty of immense charm, had travelled a lot, was well educated and had vigour, originality, intelligence, independence in mind and money, and physical stamina. She had hoped to be a social reformer in the colony, improving conditions for the women convicts, and had discussed this with Elizabeth Fry before she left England. A Ladies' Society for Prison Reform of Female Prisoners was formed, but did not last. Lady Jane was appalled at conditions for the women, but when she tried to help, newspapers accused her of 'gloating out of morbid curiosity'. She was very disturbed by such public attack, for she did care about the women and had hoped to be able to help them.

One of her official visits with her husband to the Female Factory in Hobart did leave laughter behind to echo through the next 150 years. They were accompanied on the visit by the Reverend Mr Bedford, a clergyman with a reputation for being outstandingly long-winded. The women, drawn up in rows to listen to official speeches, gave both Sir John and Lady Franklin a reasonable reception. As soon as Mr Bedford began to orate they produced a barrage of coughing. It had no effect so, at a signal from their leader, the women turned their backs, bent down, threw their skirts over their heads and began a loud, rhythmical slapping of bare backsides. This 'bottoms-up' treatment was most effective: the livid Mr Bedford ceased to speak! It had proved to be a most dramatic conversation-stopper.[2]

Jane Griffin was born in London in 1791, the middle one of three daughters of a wealthy merchant of Huguenot stock. Her mother and only brother died when Jane was very young. The girls attended a small boarding school in Chelsea and learned reading, writing, sums and tables, the Globes, dancing, catechism, French and embroidery. Jane always loved learning and was determined to be well educated. At the age of 20 she had drawn up for herself a quite fearsome plan for the employment of time and improvement of the mind. This included an hour before breakfast engaged in mental exercise not suitable for other times, and after breakfast three hours spent on logic, religious study, history, Latin, French or Italian. This daunting schedule did not prevent her from devoting afternoons to 'pursuing useful information'. Evenings, she felt, were the proper time for relaxing, for conversation, needlework, music and light reading. The Hobart ladies so many years later had reason to shudder at her idea of 'An Evening at Government House'.

It was as usual for young ladies to keep a journal as it was for them to paint gentle watercolours and play a few delicate airs on the pianoforte. Jane had started a journal when very young and had written 200 of them without ever tiring of setting down her thoughts. She was also an enthusiastic letter-writer, so much so that almost 2000 of her letters are available in transcript in various libraries. She was not one of the sketchy 'having a wonderful time, wish you were here' kind of correspondents. Her letters covered many, many pages; amazingly, in her extremely full life, she found time always for her letters and her journals.

There are many letters in the archives of the Hobart State Library and some would seem to support the popular view of her as Sir John's right hand.[3] In one letter to her sister Mary in London, Jane was delighted to relate that she was now being consulted by the Governor to such a degree that she was present in the library when the new Constitution for the colony was decided, and that draft dispatches were often submitted to her for suggestions or alterations. She begged her sister to tell nobody of this; not even their father who might, in his pride, talk about this secret matter. Jane begged also that her sister not form an opinion of her as having too high a regard for herself, but she derived enormous satisfaction from helping her husband in this way. 'My mind,' she wrote, 'is always on the stretch. I am greatly in need of relaxation and a change of scene and its accompanying cessation of ordinary and extraordinary duties.'

She was a passionate and persistent traveller and remained so all her life, having first succumbed to the travel virus in 1814 when, Napoleon being safely in exile in Elba, the wealthy Mr Griffin had taken his three daughters abroad for two years. In Geneva there had been balls, parties and mountain climbing; many social engagements in Italy, much sightseeing; and always, time to write in her journals.

There were plenty of admirers for Jane, and some proposals, but she was in no hurry to marry, cherishing her independence. Peter Mark Roget (who would later produce his invaluable *Roget's Thesaurus*) was a special friend. They were thought to be sure to marry, but it never happened. When she was 30 and heard that Roget had married someone else she professed to be heartbroken, but had said the same of another uncommitted romance in Switzerland. She often wrote in her journal about her great longing for marriage, yet turned down suitors, and then complained that this made her brother-in-law very angry.

Another admirer was Mr James Colquhoun, a young surgeon about to depart for India, who begged Jane to wait for him and to give him a lock of her hair as a keepsake. She was almost 30 then and told him she was too old for him and that he must not write, but find someone else. In her journal she wrote: 'I am becoming a bluestocking and will not now marry. In any case my indifferent health is a reasonable objection against marriage.' A tough spirit went with this seemingly frail body, which was yet able to accomplish miracles in the way of hard travelling, and Jane lived until 1875.

In London Jane became friendly with another young bluestocking, Eleanor Porden, who had become a literary figure after the publication of a very long, religious poem, *The Veil*.[4] Jane described her as a short, plain, stout young woman with nothing of pedantry or pretension in her manner. They enjoyed each other's company immensely and were able to converse on literary subjects together with great pleasure.

Jane had visited the Deptford Naval Depot where an expedition was being fitted out for the North Pole, to be led by Captain Buchan. There she met, and very much enjoyed talking to, Lieutenant John Franklin, a member of the Arctic exploration team. She was delighted later to know that her friend Eleanor and Franklin (now Captain) were to be married. She was in Germany at the time, but was back in England next year when their daughter was born.

John Franklin, a much loved and respected man, was not a romantic figure, being stout and bald, fairly humourless and deeply religious. A very kind man with a strong sense of duty, he was becoming a little deaf and financially had little but his pay as a naval officer. Eleanor Porden loved him nonetheless and brought with her to her marriage a good portion of the world's goods, her rich father having died and left all his estate to his adored only daughter.

She was well endowed in everything but health and became very frail before the birth of her daughter, also Eleanor, in London in June 1824. John Franklin had been frequently absent, preparing for a second Arctic expedition. Eleanor was glad when it was delayed, because it gave her more of his company and she must certainly have suspected she would not see him again once he had sailed. She embroidered a flag for him for his ship. Jane Griffin gave him a silver pencil with ready-pointed leads and his crest engraved on the seal at the head, and also some fur gloves.

Eleanor had been told some months before that she had tuberculosis, but made light of this and insisted she was getting better. Both pretended to believe this, and Franklin sailed away. Eleanor died a week later and the baby was taken to live with Franklin's sister. When Jane saw the small Eleanor she considered her 'to be so like her father that it is like looking at Captain Franklin through the wrong end of a telescope'.

Franklin, born in 1786, had trained as a midshipman with Matthew Flinders in the *Investigator* and was a nephew of Flinders's wife. In 1819 he had been part of a land expedition across Canada to the Arctic, and after returning from the second expedition he became a much-decorated and popular public figure. His first wife had sometimes tried to 'tease' him into being a little less rigid, but his friends judged him to be a most sensitive, courteous, honest and lovable man. Women apparently found his personality as appealing as his heroic reputation. Franklin called often at the Griffin household, bringing a gift of reindeer tongues and fur moccasins for Jane and her sisters.

A second wife, also literary, intelligent and well-to-do, would obviously suit him well. Jane, now 37, did not shilly-shally, but accepted his proposal.

Marriage to Franklin suited her in every way. She undoubtedly loved his way of life with its many opportunities for travel. Her last journey as a spinster had been to Russia, with a large family party, to join Franklin who was making an official visit. He was feted everywhere, a guest of honour at state balls, received by the Empress.

Their wedding trip was to Paris, accompanied by two cousins. This was not unusual, but Jane's sudden submissiveness was. From Russia she had written him an extraordinary letter promising she would always be a submissive wife and advising him to keep the letter safe so that if at any future time she should become rebellious he could produce the letter. 'I have made you infinitely obliged to me for furnishing you with this valuable document.'

She was also quixotic enough to refuse a marriage settlement from him — though he had little money of his own to offer, his inheritance from his first wife being his main source of income. Jane, who had £7000 of her own before marriage and a settlement of £3000 from her father, would have given the lot to Franklin, capital and income, if he had so wished.

The little Eleanor was then aged 6½ and Jane tried hard to become a good mother, but the girl did not respond happily. She adored her father and at times seemed to dislike Jane intensely. Franklin received a knighthood soon afterwards and later resumed naval service in the Mediterranean. Jane joined him with two companions, an elderly American couple, both intrepid travellers like herself. With them she went to Spain, Egypt, the Holy Land and North Africa, 'where we lived very higgledy-piggledy in a small Moorish house with no windows, open to the sky and sun of the roof'. They were plagued by bugs, mosquitoes and foul smells. She visited Greece and

Turkey, where she and her friends lived in a tent of skins and carpets and Turkish gipsy women went to see her and 'some stooped to turn up my petticoats to see for themselves if I wore trowsers which I took great pains to show them I did'.

Back in England the Franklins were received in the Pavilion at Brighton by King William IV and later, when for the first time in thirty-four years there was no naval position for him, Sir John was offered the Lieutenant-Governorship of Van Diemen's Land.[5] They sailed in August 1836, leaving Jane's father (almost 80) and her sisters desolate at losing her. With them went young Eleanor, Franklin's Private Secretary, Captain Alexander Maconochie, RN, his wife and six children, an ADC and some staff and two of Franklin's nieces, Sophia Cracroft and Mary Franklin.

Governor Arthur had been considered autocratic and difficult and the people, glad to see him go, gave the Franklins a most cordial reception. The love affair did not last long, particularly in their feelings towards Lady Jane. Her analytical mind, her vitality, Sir John's complete faith in her and the fact that she had money of her own gave her quite startling independence of action. She achieved many 'firsts'. She was the first woman to climb Mount Wellington, the first one to go into the wild country in the south-west between Lake St Clair and the west coast, and when she visited the mainland she was the first woman to ride overland from Melbourne to Sydney (though Janet Templeton and Sarah Docker had both overlanded with their husbands and families, travelling the reverse route).

In 1840 Jane made a trip to South Australia. There was heavy rain during her sojourns on deck, and rats and mice raced through the cabins at night, when the lamps were put out, in search of water. She was stoical, even humorous, about both.

Almost everything she did attracted attention, most of it unfavourable. Her effort to rid Van Diemen's Land of snakes brought a particularly violent reaction. She loathed snakes and felt she would do the public a service by offering to pay, from her own pocket, 1 shilling per head for every dead snake brought in to police stations. There was near rioting as convicts downed tools to set about this lucrative task of catching snakes. Jane is said to have paid out £600 of her own money, bounty on 12 000 reptiles. She was accused of subverting convict discipline, which of course upset her, but she did admit that perhaps she had been rather reckless and suggested that tea, sugar and tobacco should be given in place of money. The Great Snake Removal plan was not judged a success and faded away, but one irate settler whose convict labour had enthusiastically joined in the snake hunt took an unkind revenge by sending Lady Jane an enormous St Valentine's Day card with a dead snake attached.

Meanwhile a bitter power-struggle was brewing in Hobart, with Government House its centre. The Colonial Secretary, Captain John Montague, had been appointed by the previous Governor, Arthur, his wife's uncle. He clashed continually with Franklin's Private Secretary and with Franklin himself. He had a good deal of influence in colonial circles in England and sent extremely one-sided reports to English newspapers. Rows and recriminations would eventually lead to Franklin's resignation.

After a trip to New Zealand which greatly 'refreshed' her, Jane tried again to improve conditions for the convict women and was again attacked in the newspapers, one declaring that 'the wife of Sir John is but a man in petticoats'. She was greatly distressed, for she did care about the women. Her emigration scheme however, *was* successful. She had bought 243 hectares of land in the Huon Valley, in the area named Franklin after her. Detractors claimed that she had been *granted* the land by the Governor, but originally it had been a grant for services rendered to John Price, Superintendent of Convicts. She purchased it from him and went to Port Davey to buy a small vessel (about 35–40 tonnes) 'for the service of my new settlement on the Huon'. By 1839 the scheme was well established. Allotments were large, terms were easy and rations were supplied, to be repaid in kind or produce. Many of the Huon settlers were Methodists and Jane built a wooden chapel for them.

She was also behind the establishment of an educational college in 1840. (After many romantic ups and downs and partings and meanderings, its principal, the Reverend J. R. Gell of Rugby and Cambridge, married Jane's step-daughter Eleanor.) Jane's last act in Van Diemen's Land was to make over 162 hectares of land she had bought near Hobart, with the small museum she had built on it, to the trustees of the future college. A scientific society had been formed which met each fortnight and Jane built them a small, stone museum in the design of a Greek temple, planted a garden about it and gave it a Greek name, Acanthe, Vale of Flowers. After the Franklins' departure the building gradually became derelict. In 1926 an Act of Parliament transferred it to Hobart City Council and in 1948 the Art Society of Tasmania began to administer it as an art gallery. Only fifteen minutes from the city, the miniature parthenon in its native garden is a gracious memorial to an intelligent and spirited woman.

Jane left her imprint on Tasmania in many ways, including its name. She declared that Van Diemen's Land had a 'very awkward' sound and suggested it be renamed Tasmania. During their regime the Franklins welcomed many scientists and explorers to Hobart, including Darwin on the *Beagle*.[6] During her visit to South Australia Jane went to Port Lincoln and paid £250, out of her own pocket, for a memorial to Matthew Flinders to be erected on a cliff-top site. When she came to Melbourne she was delighted to be given an address of welcome signed by sixty-nine civil officers, magistrates, clergy, merchants, landowners and stock proprietors, who expressed the hope that she would be impressed by the appearance of Melbourne after only eighteen months of existence. In New South Wales the keen traveller went up to the Hunter River district and was very happy to meet Anna Josepha King, widow of the former Governor (as boys, Sir John and Philip Gidley King had been midshipmen on Flinders's *Investigator*).

The Franklins' last months in Hobart were not happy, for Montague had gone to England and was making trouble there.[7] Local papers were vicious. Franklin asked to be recalled, but a new Governor had already been appointed and arrived before Sir John had received official notification. They returned to England and soon Franklin, although too old for it, was away on his third Arctic expedition. He never returned. Jane was busy begging the government to send relief expeditions and trying to fund some herself. Gell was in England; he and Eleanor wanted to marry and demanded money from Jane. Gell complained that Franklin had made no provision for his future son-in-law. Jane had power of attorney and had offered them a good allowance, but they wanted more. She wrote to Franklin:

> Mr Gell is one of the Curates of St Martin's and has this curacy, with £100 he has from his father, about £50 from the Gospel Society and a small fixed income of his own to which I add an allowance to make it up to £500 per year until the time of your return.

That would then have been a handsome sum, but for the rest of her life Jane was plagued by their demands for money.

Jane's father had died and, believing her to be well-off (he had sent £5000 to her in Tasmania), had left his money to a grandson. After it was learned that the entire exploration party had perished, Gell demanded that Jane return *all* the income she had received from the estate since Franklin's death. At 58, she had been a widow for twelve years before the last mementoes of Franklin were brought back. She gave them to the Admiralty.

She spent much of her life after that travelling (Hawaii, Rio, Canada and the United States being among her last visits) and occasionally dabbling in spiritualism. After her death in 1875, aged 84, the devoted niece Sophia Cracroft, who had been her close companion, wrote about

> ... her clearness of perception, strong reasoning powers, delicacy, power of analysis, tenacity of purpose, power of disentanglement, ability to describe, enthusiasm, sympathy, longing for truth, intelligence and passionate love of justice.

Few people in her lifetime, other than her family and Sir John, had given such recognition to Lady Jane—an independent spirit.

Lola Montez

WOMEN ON THE GOLDFIELDS

On a low hill close to Castlemaine, in Victoria, wind and rain have weathered the few whole headstones that remain of the Pennyweight Flat Children's Cemetery.¹ Most of the graves are only mounds under the grass; some have borders of broken stones. It is a gentle, pretty place with birds and hilltop breezes, a reminder of one of Australia's minor tragedies, brought about by gold fever.

More than 200 children were buried there who died of the goldrush diseases, fevers and infections contained in the putrid water which spread pollution. For the women who went with their men to the Victorian goldfields, some of them walking from Melbourne, helping to push barrows and pull carts, taking children with them, Pennyweight Flat was a sad end to family life. Most of the children were very young: in memory of Elizabeth Corbis who died 30 January 1855, aged 18 months; Hugh James Brierley who died 26 January 1853, aged 14 months; John Skillicorn, in memory of his daughter Mary who died 8 February 1855, aged 18 months. One child was 8, another 4, the majority under two.

The goldrush brought about more social changes in Victoria in a short time than any other event in history. In 1851 Victoria's population was just over 77 000; and it was about 95 000 a year later. Within three more years it had increased to about 300 000 as ships arrived from every one of the world's ports and treasure-seekers flocked from other states. Nothing was so important as gold. Shops, banks, businesses and properties were almost deserted as men went off, leaving wives and families behind them and sometimes a note, 'Gone to the diggings'.

Deserted wives in Melbourne grouped together to share houses for their own protection.[2] A canvas town sprang up on the south side of the Yarra River and women lived there in tents, some almost penniless, wondering if they would ever see husbands again, taking in washing and doing housework to support themselves.

It was the same in the town of Geelong. The *Geelong Advertiser* commented: 'Geelong is mad, stark, staring, gold mad. The number of disconsolate wives or as they are called "grass widows" and their families is astonishing.'[3] And later:

> *Some rather ridiculous scenes begin to show themselves down here. Young misses whose papas have been to Ballarat, begin to appear in new bonnets and dresses and, with parasols, strut about like Indiarubber dolls. They would certainly go the whole animal were there not a severe check to their presumption and pride in the fact that all the nice young men and the majority of old bachelors have left town. Several once respectable and sedate matrons are going it strong in beautiful new silk dresses with the additional advantage of*

being strangely perfumed which with their gaudy dresses gives them the appearance of small walking flower gardens. Another class of inferior stamp may sometimes be seen in some of the Inns here, with a small roll of notes in one hand and a pot of half and half or a ½ pint of gin in the other, treating all and sundry who come their way.[4]

Where the men went, many of the women went too, living on the goldfields in tents with their husbands, putting a mat on the floor, sheets on a camp bed, desperately trying to maintain gentility in very difficult circumstances.[5] And for every respectable woman on the goldfields there were two of the other kind, temporary brides and soon-flitting housekeepers who went when the money went. Diggers' weddings were an uproarious feature of life in Melbourne as men back from the goldfields, flourishing champagne bottles, lolled in carriages with brightly dressed brides as they raced along Collins Street. Some lodging houses in the town would supply a young lady who, for a 'consideration', would act the role of a bride. Carriage and footmen would also be provided for the bridegrooms, who lit cigars with banknotes, waved flags, dressed ostentatiously and behaved outrageously. The 'brides' enjoyed it enormously.

Women were scarce on the goldfields, but they were there, in the proportion of one to every four men. They rocked their babies' cradles, they rocked the gold cradles, they were 'digger-esses', they were lodging-house keepers, cooks and nurses, brothel-owners and good-time girls. There were some genuine 'ladies', among them Ellen Clacy[6], a super-achiever who, in just under a year, travelled from England as companion to her younger brother and returned with a brand new husband, with memories of miners and flooded creeks, rough living on the diggings, bushrangers and a satisfying quantity of gold. She also had the manuscript of a book written on the homeward journey and published, with astonishing speed, on her return: *A Lady's Visit to the Gold Diggings of Australia 1852–53 Written on the spot by Mrs Charles Clacy.*

This small (she calls herself 'a pocket edition'), lively and obviously impetuous young woman who decided quite suddenly to accompany her brother to Melbourne was an extraordinary vision on the goldfields. He had just left school and she, protective sister not much older than he, would go too. There were, apparently, no restraints from guardian or parent. Their ship arrived on 22 August 1852 and after a few days of buying and packing she was off to find gold with her brother, four other young men who had formed a party with him on board ship and several newcomers—two Germans going to Forest Creek with a dray, two Frenchmen with diggers' kits, two surgeons with medical kit; there were also three packhorses and a dray for Ellen's group.

The men carried their swags of personal belongings, knife or tomahawk in belt, chamois leather bags tucked away for the gold they hoped to bring back. Ellen rode on the dray, a delightfully nonchalant picture of self-reliant womanhood. She was walled in by the canvas and poles of the tent, had a bag of flour as a backrest and a large cheese for a footstool, and was 'tolerably comfortable'. Her garb was unfashionable, though appropriate, 'a dress of common dark blue serge, a felt wide-awake hat and an enveloping 'waterproof coat'.

The road to the diggings was terrible—bogs, deep ruts, water-filled holes, tree stumps—scarcely a road at all. It rained almost incessantly and Ellen spent several uncomfortable nights sleeping, fully clothed, in a partitioned-off corner of her brother's tent. Eleven days after leaving Melbourne the party had established a camp at the diggings. The weather was fine when they reached Bendigo and Ellen found it an exciting and memorable scene, like a sandy plain where the trees had all been cut down and the earth was 'one vast unbroken succession of countless gravel pits'. Men's heads continually popped up and down from the holes. There was the noise of swaying cradles, sounds of pick and shovel; a busy hum from thousands of tents above which fluttered the flags of every nation.

They went 8 kilometres further on and pitched their own tents at Eagle Hawk Gully. (Ellen seems to have had no qualms as to the propriety of a single young lady travelling and camping with five young men.) Most of the next day was spent in walking to and from Bendigo to obtain licences. Ellen, 'not a good housekeeper', nevertheless did most of the cooking, buying half a sheep at a time from the butcher (who would not sell less) for 8 shillings and baking it outside the tent in a large camp oven on a tripod. Her first effort at gold-washing delighted her, yielding nearly two pennyweights of gold-dust, worth about 6 or 7 shillings.

On Saturday 2 October they hit a 'pocket' and brought up 'nugget after nugget from the dirty soil, five pounds weight of gold'. They worked until dark and gave up reluctantly, because they would have to wait until Monday to find out whether the strike would continue. (No work was done on the goldfields on Sundays.) Their luck held out and Ellen did her full share of the work and received her full share of the rewards. Like other seekers, they wanted more. Hearing of a good new strike further up the field at Iron Bark Gully, they struck camp and went there.

Here they encountered a sad child and Ellen's record of the meeting, written in the middle of the 19th century, rings soberly through to the present. Out for a late afternoon walk, Ellen and Frank, the much-respected oldest of their group, saw in a quiet place beneath two trees a small homemade tent: a blanket suspended over a rope and fastened to the ground. A 10-year-old girl sat on a rock by the opening, fingers busy on coarse green gauze to make a digger's veil, protection against the dust. She offered Frank a veil, and looked imploring as she said 'I haven't sold one this week'. Frank took one but returned it, which upset her pride and she offered homemade candles instead. She made veils and candles herself in an effort to earn money to feed her grandfather who lay, very ill, in the tent:

> *He's asleep now. He sleeps more than he did. He's killed hisself digging for gold and he never got none. And he says he'll dig till he dies.*[7]

Prophetic words, for the next morning the grandfather was dead in the tent with the child, awake and moaning, beside him.

Her story was not unfamiliar on the goldfields. Father, mother, grandfather and the child Jessie had been at the diggings for a year. Father had had an accident and died and the mother had not long survived him, leaving Jessie and the old man alone. For her, he had worked long hours with no success, vowing: 'we shall be rich and Jessie a fine lady before I die'.

The child's story touched them deeply.

> *I* never *left him—I* never *neglected him. When I waked in the morning I thought him asleep. I made my fire. I crept softly about to make his gruel for breakfast, and I took it him and found him dead—dead!*

Money was left with the butcher to have the old man buried and Jessie accompanied the party on their goldfields travels until they were back in Melbourne. There, Ellen arranged for the girl to live as companion and mother's help with a respectable family.

Her own future had changed dramatically. On the way back to town one of the young men, Octavius, had met his 33-year-old uncle. The latter had left England eight years previously for South Australia and not been heard from since: imagined dead. This lively gentleman, tall and sun-bronzed and handsome, a wonderful raconteur and bold adventurer, had then accompanied them to Melbourne, had survived with them a bushranger's attempted robbery (knives, tomahawks, pistols and ropes had been used). His traveller's tales had enthralled Ellen. She is most reticent throughout the book in giving personal details (except her small size, for she almost drowned when she stumbled into a water-logged excavation only 1·5 metres deep). He *must* have been the husband with whom she arrived in England.

> *And now two out of the three weeks of our party's stay in Melbourne had expired, during which a change had made my brother's protection no longer needed by me. My* wedding trip *was to be to England, and the marriage to take place and myself and* caro sposo *to leave Australia before my brother departed for the Ovens diggings.*

A 'sufficiency' of gold, a fiancé rapidly become husband and three months of the kind of adventures which scarcely another young lady from England could expect ever to enjoy were all achieved by Ellen in less than one year, as well as a return voyage from Australia to England—a near-miraculous accomplishment!

The most notorious woman to appear on the Australian goldfields was certainly Maria Dolores Eliza Rosanna Gilbert.[8] She had other names: Mrs Betty James; Betty Gilbert; the Countess Marie von Landsfeld; Mrs Heald, wife of a rich Life Guards officer in London; Mrs Patrick Hull. All the names were submerged in the tempestuous personality of the woman who also called herself Señora Maria de los Dolores Porris Y Montez.

Lola Montez left a colourful smear across goldfields history; she shocked bishops but entranced miners in Bendigo, Ballarat and Castlemaine; she both delighted and stormed at audiences in Melbourne and Sydney. In Adelaide her performance was accorded a unique tribute—'a unanimous turnout of the Free Masons of South Australia in full regalia'. They presented her with several valuable pieces of jewellery, a splendid insurance against her inevitable periods of financial despair.

Lola was born in Limerick, Ireland, in 1818 and as a baby was taken to India by her very young mother, who had been seduced at 13 and later married by Ensign Edward Gilbert of the British 44th Regiment. He died in India of cholera and young Mrs Gilbert soon married Major John Craigie, later General Sir John Craigie, Adjutant-General of the British Indian Army. Lola's mother, who claimed to belong to a Spanish Grandee family, sent the little girl to boarding school in England and did not see her again until she paid a visit to England when the girl was 18. A picture of Lola Montez at 18 shows a deliciously beautiful and wistfully beguiling girl, enormous dark eyes, dark hair down to her waist.

Delighted with her enchanting daughter, the mother told her she had arranged a marriage with a 60-year-old Indian supreme court judge. The girl rebelled and took refuge with another of her mother's admirers, Lieutenant Thomas James, also an Indian Army officer visiting England, whose 'fatherly' interest soon changed. They were married in 1837 and two years later went to India, where Lola (Betty James) became the regimental beauty. James, however, was a womaniser and eloped with another army wife. Her stepfather offered her a home, but her mother did not welcome such close competition with her own charms. The General gave the girl a cheque for £1000, which she used to go to England and take the first steps towards a sensational career combining theatrical and amatory talents.

James brought an action for judicial separation, the granting of which meant that, under British law, she would never be able to marry (legally) again while he lived. (It may have been James from whom she contracted syphilis, which meant recurring health troubles for Lola and for some of her many lovers.) After a sojourn in Spain during which she took lessons in Spanish dancing, she returned to London as Donna Lola Montez. She was graceful, fiery, voluptuous, and her dancing evoked rapturous acclaim. Her stage acting—for she fancied herself an accomplished actress—did not.

It was the 'spider dance' which brought most fame and most disapproval. It also brought the crowds in Australia and was often substituted if her acting performance had failed. She made it more or less 'exotic' as seemed suitable. Because of it, in Melbourne, a magistrate had been asked to issue an order for her arrest. In that city George Coppin, a rival theatrical manager, himself performed a Lola Montez burlesque and wrote a new verse for the popular Billy Barlow ballad:

> *When famed Lola Montez for spiders did look*
> *I took a leaf out of her very blue book.*
> *For the lady considers she's something to show*
> *Not at all like the spider of Billy Barlow.*

She had arrived in Australia after many successes and disasters in Europe and America. Her affair with 60-year-old Ludwig I of Bavaria, during which she had interfered in both religious and political matters, had ended badly. Her career often swung between farce and melodrama, an instance of the latter being an altercation with the editor of the *Ballarat Times* when she rushed at him with a horsewhip and he took his own whip to her.

For a while she was 'Queen of the Goldfields', and sometimes miners responded to her invitation to throw gold on to the stage. Often there was standing room only at performances by this notorious woman with the magnificent eyes and the sinuous movements. When she sailed back to America she was able to take a sizeable hoard of gold, jewels and cash as souvenirs of success. Her co-actor and companion vanished overboard during the voyage and Lola, found in a faint, said that he had tried to grab the moneybags and then jumped. Her story was accepted.

She continued to act and to travel; she became religious and went on tour with a clergyman, to read his writings. Her jewels had been sold for food and lodging. In January 1861, aged only 42, Mrs Eliza Gilbert died (probably of syphilis) and was buried in a Brooklyn cemetery.

In her fondness for the whip as a deterrent to intractable male behaviour, Lola Montez had a rival on the goldfields. Mrs Buntine (Mother Buntine, Mrs Bunting) was a woman of formidable physical size. William Howitt (1855), in his shrewd and wide-ranging account of the diversities of life then, offers this vignette:

> *an enormously fat woman whose husband is a storekeeper . . . known as a sly grog seller but sets the law at defiance . . . she rode on horseback about the diggings and was especially ambitious to be sketched in equestrian character. Nothing can exceed her dignity or bulk except it were a Turkish dome or a steam boiler on horseback . . . she drove down to Melbourne with the Gold Escort with a pair of pistols in her belt at her capacious waist and told the troopers with the Escort she would protect them in case of attack from bushrangers.*[9]

She was a Scots girl, born Agnes Davidson.[10] She migrated with her parents and family and in Melbourne in 1840 married recently bereaved Hugh Buntine, whose wife had died of typhus while their ship was in quarantine in Sydney. To his five children she added six of her own.

The Buntines were Gippsland pioneers, both as tough as the newly opened country. They had a large run near Bruthen, conducted the Bush Inn there and operated various stores.

Mrs Buntine became a bullock driver and carrier who never missed a chance of trade. She was also a carrier operating with packhorses between Melbourne and the Bendigo goldfields. When a road was put through to the isolated settlement at Walhalla, she was one of the first to use it. It was in this area she took her bullock whip to a drunken digger who had insulted a girl.

Obviously as good as any man, Mrs Buntine took the first packhorse team into Walhalla, was the first to slaughter a beast there and acted as butcher for some years. After her husband's death in 1867 she continued the bullock teams, considering that there was better money to be made there than in anything else.

'Everybody knew her and everyone had some anecdote to relate,' Howitt wrote. One story is that at the age of 56 she married again, this time to a farmer called Michael Mallett said to have been 29 years old!

Georgiana Molloy

WOMEN IN THE WEST I

Georgiana Molloy

The history of European settlement of Australia's south-west coast was very different from that of the eastern states.[1] In 1827 Captain James Stirling had visited the western coast of 'New Holland' in HMS *Success*. On his return he gave such an enthusiastic report that the British Government had decided to found not another penal settlement, but a new colony. Promises of vast land grants in what seemed like a new Garden of Eden tempted some unlikely settlers. Ladies and gentlemen came to the empty land in search of prosperity, few of them used to manual labour, not dreaming that the future would be formed by their own hands. (There were no convicts; there were servants and labourers, but many of them would want their own land, and soon.) With such a prospect dangled before them, the ladies and gentlemen packed and sailed on a dream.

They came, many of them, in response to a government promise. In London an advertisement appeared, in December 1828, regarding a proposed new settlement on the west coast of New Holland:

> *Settlers will have no purchase money to pay for their lands nor will they be chargeable for any rent whatever. Their grants will be conveyed to them in fee simple and will descend to their assignees or heirs forever, thereby affording them the satisfaction of knowing that their labour will be wholly expended on their own property, and that the results of their patient endeavours will be enjoyed by their children and their names transmitted with such estates to distant posterity.*[2]

HMSS *Sulphur* and *Parmelia* arrived in 1829. On 2 May that year, Captain Fremantle took possession of the country there for Great Britain.[3]

The unrest and dissatisfaction that follow war were felt throughout England, and the aftermath of the Napoleonic Wars, now long over, was a superior class of unemployed. Hundreds of naval and military officers, husbands and sons, were out of a job or had been placed on half-pay. They came from good families and many had been in one of the services for most of their lives. Some would have had knowledge of the land, but from the perspective of a 'gentleman', not a labourer with dirty hands. Their wives and daughters were 'ladies', sheltered and gentle creatures educated at home (though not too academically), deft at 'arranging' things that others had grown or washed or cooked or carried—flowers, linen cupboards, preserves on pantry shelves. They embroidered, painted woodland scenes, played piano accompaniment. Physical labour was a stroll to the village, a walk to church or a wander along forest tracks collecting specimens from Nature.

People like this were to be Western Australia's first white settlers, sailing on a wave of optimism to visions of vast acres in a new land where life might be a little uncomfortable at first, but must soon assume its familiar, well-bred shape. They came of their own accord, under no pressures except economic ones; some of the men restless and anxious to try something new, with England so unsettled after a long period of war. They had families which must be provided with a better future than England could offer; or they wished to marry and establish families. Their wives came, less eagerly perhaps, and more impressed by the vast distance that would now separate them from parents and relatives and friends.

Georgiana Molloy was one of the wives.[4] Like so many of the well-bred Englishwomen who were Swan River pioneers, she came from refined surroundings to *nothing* except the promise of land, a future that *might* be splendid and the warm thoughts of a family of her own to cherish. In her case, as in many others, that family—too many babies produced too regularly—certainly shortened her life.

Miss Georgiana Kennedy was 24 when she agreed to marry Captain John Molloy, a dashing and well-regarded war hero twice her age.[5] She came from Carlisle, near the Scots border, and was a deeply religious and thoughtful girl; a favourite pastime was to have long, long discussions on religious thoughts and beliefs. Two of her best friends had married clergymen and she often stayed with them, revelling in continual dialogues about Church and Faith. Her belief in God would later help her to survive many hardships and personal tragedies. Had not the attractive Captain appeared in her life, she would perhaps have married one of the many available clergymen seeking well-brought up wives, and dedicated the rest of her life to the Church.

Molloy had been well educated, with money and influence expended on his behalf. There were no apparent relatives, but there was an intriguing air of mystery as to his background. 'Handsome Jack', as his service friends called him, was rumoured to be the natural child of one of George II's roistering sons. Frederick, Duke of York, was credited with having fathered him.

The new colony being established with much enthusiasm interested Captain Molloy, who had long felt it was time to marry and establish a family and a future. He had known Georgiana for some time and the quiet and thoughtful Miss Kennedy seemed to be an admirable choice for a wife. Having made many inquiries as to the possibilities of settlement on the Swan River, in the summer of 1829 he wrote to Georgiana, then holidaying in Scotland, and proposed marriage. He also outlined his plans for emigrating.

A great deal of soul- and heart-searching must have been needed before she wrote her acceptance. It was not romance of the highly passionate kind, nor was Georgiana being swept off her feet. She soon became devoted to her John, however, vowing in a shipboard letter to friends that he was a dear creature and she would not exchange him for £10 000 a year and a great mansion in a civilised country. When he received her acceptance Molloy, in London, immediately began to make formal preparations for the voyage, engaging servants, buying stock and farm implements. Then he travelled north for the wedding.

After her father's death, when she was about 16, Georgiana's family had moved from Carlisle to Rugby, where the two boys might have a good education. Georgiana did not seem particularly close to her two sisters and spent as much time as possible staying with her special friends, the Dunlops, in Dunbartonshire. Georgiana and John were married there in August 1829 by the Reverend Robert Story, husband of her friend Helen Dunlop. On the way back to London they spent several days with her family in Rugby, so that Georgiana could make her farewells and pack personal possessions.

Very soon the new Mrs Molloy was in London with her husband and they were booked to sail on the *Warrior*, 489 tonnes, carrying 166 passengers.[6]

A portrait of Georgiana painted about that time shows a

fashionable figure in a dark, off-the-shoulder gown, a serene and beautiful young woman, wide-browed, her thick blonde hair worn high on top with long loops over each ear.

When she shopped in London, she forswore fashion for practicality. She had never been inclined to the frivolities of life and the gowns she bought were all plain, hems and tucks their only trimming; her bonnets, too, were plain and practical. One of the things she would dearly have loved to take with her was a good piano, for she loved music and was an excellent pianist. Her other particular interest was in 'botanising' and this she did indulge by adding many packets of garden seeds to the long shopping list, which included twelve months' supply of provisions.

When the Molloys sailed on 22 October 1829 they had as fellow passengers (though travelling steerage and not first, as they were) four of the Bussell family, who were to be neighbours and fellow pioneers in Western Australia. Another son, three daughters and Mrs Bussell would follow when a home was ready for them.[7] The Bussells were good company on a rough and tedious voyage during which Georgiana suffered from violent seasickness and, as she was pregnant, probably from morning sickness as well.

The Turners were also on board, a large and jolly family who would later be excellent and generous neighbours to both Molloys and Bussells. Mr Turner had been a successful builder in London, but because of the general trade slump had decided to sell his business and emigrate. With his tidy capital he would be able to build up a neat little empire in the colony.

The Turners were almost two families: James and his wife Maria, the eldest children Ann (18) and William (16), and six smaller Turners for whom Ann was old enough to act as second mother. The large party, with servants, luggage and household supplies, had the biggest and best accommodation on the *Warrior*. Even so, they found their cabins cramped and in his journal James Turner complained of the dirt and confusion everywhere on the ship, and the poor lighting. He was glad that he and his wife and children were all small, which made things easier for them.

Although he travelled in superior style and had more money

than any of his upper-crust fellow passengers, owing to his inferior social position Mr Turner was never fully accepted by them as an equal. His good temper and sense of humour allowed him to accept without apparent resentment that he was 'not quite a gentleman'.

Georgiana (who later described Mr Turner as 'a jolly little tradesman') would not have chosen him to talk to or stroll with on deck, but she found the young Bussell men, when they came up from steerage, were very good companions. They were, of course, much more of her own age group than was her husband. To young men in their twenties, the Captain must have seemed quite ancient, in their own father's age group. Charles Bussell described Molloy as 'rather nestorious for so young a wife', likening him to an Homeric hero noted for his age, his experience and his wisdom.[8] Writing about Georgiana, he said she was a delightful 'acquisition' to the ship's society, 'rather inclined to the romantic and delighted to have anyone with whom she can contemplate the sublimity of a night scene or expatiate upon the beauties of this or that piece of poetry'.

Cape Town provided the Molloys with a most enjoyable sojourn on land. They enjoyed the hospitality of several of the Captain's former army friends and made some short journeys into the country. Georgiana loved the tropical plants and laid out £7 17s 6d on seeds and shrubs, including watsonias, lilies, oleanders and Cape gooseberries.

When the Molloys arrived in March 1830 at recently named Fremantle, there were already a few pre-cut wooden houses, but most of the accommodation was in tents. Georgiana was in the late stages of her first pregnancy and found the heat and the glare from sun and sand very trying. She was anxious to settle quickly, and next day they went by boat 22 kilometres up the Swan River to the settlement in Perth, feeling that the sooner they could obtain their broad acres, the sooner they could get this shining future under way. But although it was only eleven months since Captain Stirling (now Governor of this new colony), his wife and the first settlers had arrived on the *Parmelia*, the Molloys found that the best land along the Swan

River had already been allocated. It was the first of many frustrations and disappointments.

Georgiana found Perth a much more congenial place than Fremantle. There were a few houses, some public offices and three very small licensed inns. A street had been cleared (St Georges Terrace), but shady trees left along one side made it pleasant. The social scene was quite lively, with its groups of former naval and military officers and their wives, many of them cousins of friends or friends of cousins. The Molloys were asked to enjoyable parties and entertainments and Georgiana found the Governor's wife, Ellen, a charming companion. Ellen had been married at 16 and had given birth to her second child soon after the *Parmelia* sailed for the Swan River. She was still only 23 and enjoyed the informality of this new life.

Parties were fun; at one given on 23 April to celebrate the King's birthday there were sixty people present, only eight of them ladies. But the weather was still hot and Georgiana was glad when in May the Molloys, the Bussells, the Turners and other families of settlers, with their servants and household belongings, sailed south on the brig *Emily Taylor*, chartered for £200. Captain Molloy had been appointed a Justice of the Peace for the southern area and had made an application for land there. In return for a capital investment of £960 10s 5½d on behalf of himself, his wife and five adult servants with three children, he was granted 12 813 acres (5185 hectares). Mr Turner's family and retainers totalled thirty; for his capital investment of £1502 he had been allotted 8110 hectares plus a further 2025 hectares. The four Bussell brothers, worth only £317 12s 11d, were granted only 2257 hectares of land.

The three families were neighbours at Augusta, the minute settlement around the coast from Cape Leeuwin at the tip of Western Australia. Not one of them was to remain there, though the Molloys stayed longest. There is nothing left now of the properties except names and memories and wild watsonias, but it is a beautiful place where the Blackwood River runs into the sea and the crash of breaking waves sometimes dims the sound of wind blowing through trees. A caravan park stands on some of James Turner's land and a plaque marks the place on the beach where the *Emily Taylor*'s passengers landed. Some of the old names can be read above graves in a small pioneer cemetery up the hill in the bush.

Seven days after they landed, Georgiana's first baby was born in a tent, in the rain, with only a servant's wife to help; but it did not live long. She was devastated and felt terribly alone. Molloy, busy with both official affairs and his land grant, was sympathetic, but this was a woman's business. The death of a child was no uncommon thing, in England or in this new land; several babies had died while they were in Perth. Georgiana grieved in silence and it was years before she felt able to put her thoughts at that time into a letter, a haunting testament:

> . . . language refused to utter what I experienced when mine died in my arms in this dreary land, with no one but Molloy near me. I thought I might have had one little bright object left to solace all the hardships and privations I suffered and have still to go through. *It was wicked and I am still not now thoroughly at peace* . . . its grave, though sodded with British clover, looks so singular and solitary in this wilderness, of which I can scarcely give you an idea.⁹

She grew to love this particular part of the country dearly, however. Their house was built close to the wide Blackwood River, with a magnificent view up the estuary to the sea. There was always a breeze and she found the climate, at least, delightful. Behind the small, two-storeyed house with its well-detached kitchen and scullery were rooms for Elijah Dawson, Molloy's former army corporal who, with his new wife, had come as their servant.

The Bussells had a small wooden house with a clay and rubble chimney. Turner's place, Albion, was set well back and was quite imposing, as he had brought out much prefabricated material. Pictures of the little settlement, painted by a Turner son, are in the historical museum at Augusta, as are Elijah Dawson's journal and several small relics of Georgiana and John Molloy.

Domestic help was a continuing problem. Men and women who had emigrated as servants naturally wanted to take up land for themselves. Often Georgiana had no help at all. By the end of 1831 she was coping with practically all the domestic work, looking after her new baby girl, Sabina, and managing to play hostess for an official visit by the Governor and his wife. She entertained them well. Charles Bussell still admired her immensely and said he could never praise her too highly. 'She is perfectly ladylike yet does not disdain the minutiae of domestic economy, an indispensable accomplishment in a settler's wife.'

Though Georgiana complained in letters to her friends about the never-ending chores, she did them efficiently. She missed the company of her women friends and tried to keep in touch by letter . . .

> I have seven letters of Molloy's relating to business to answer, besides my own; to weigh out rations, attend to baby and, although needlework of every kind both for her, Molloy and myself and servant is required, I have not touched a needle for this week. I am now exhausted and the day is uncommonly hot. I told you how it would be: I should have to take in washing and Jack carry home the clean clothes in a swill. The last of this has not yet happened but between ourselves, dear Maggie, the first is no uncommon occurrence. What goes to my heart is that dear Molloy has so much exertion bodily and mentally but I am repaid with interest when any part I perform eases his task. The Lord is good and has shown Himself to us in many wonderful instances.

Molloy was appointed Government Resident and was often away on official business. Alone at home on the baby's first birthday, Georgiana wrote with great satisfaction about the heavenly climate:

> . . . while you are burning the front breadth of your frock and the nebs of your shoes at an excellent fire of Newcastle coals I am sitting in the verandah surrounded by my little flower garden of British, Cape and Australian flowers pouring forth their odour and a variety of beautiful little birds most brilliant in plumage sporting around.

She was delighted to know that two of the Bussell girls, Bessie and Fanny, and another brother would soon arrive.

Having not enough room in the house, she arranged for them to stay in a neighbour's cottage as her guests. Fanny Bussell wrote:

> Mrs Molloy came to receive us with her little Sabina in her arms, looking so youthful and interesting. She has fitted a cottage up so nicely, a French bed and all sorts of land comforts. A vase of sweet mignonette upon the table and a large wood fire blazing. We spent a most pleasant evening.[10]

Bessie Bussell went up to the second Bussell property to look after three of the boys, while Fanny stayed at Augusta to keep house for Charles. When Georgiana was ill she helped her and looked after Sabina. The Bussells soon had a catastrophe of their own, when the new house burned down and they lost most of their belongings, clothes included. The piano was saved and placed in Georgiana's house, where it gave her great joy. Being able to play music made up in small part for the sewing she had to do and loathed. 'I stitch my fingers to the bone to keep Molloy, Sabina and myself in constant repair.' When a new baby was due, she said she had no time 'even to sew the child a cap'. Mary Dorothea was born in June 1834, a very healthy, plump and beautiful baby. Three years later there was a boy, whose birth delighted both parents. They all adored the lively little boy.

Now Georgiana had a new interest. She had received a letter from a stranger—Captain Mangles, a naturalist and a cousin of the Governor's wife, Ellen Stirling. He was in touch with all the great gardens in England and he sent her a box of seeds and asked her to collect specimens for him. She was so busy with the children, her garden and the absorbing pastime of collecting and labelling specimens, that she had scarcely time to miss neighbours, most of whom had left to take up land on the Vasse River. That spring she spent many hours wandering with the two little girls and the boy toddler, enjoying this interesting new occupation. It gave her enormous satisfaction and she was becoming a knowledgeable and capable botanist. The friendship by letter with Captain Mangles was a sharing of thoughts and interests. He sent her books, seeds, presents for the children. Her specimens always arrived in England perfectly packed and labelled. They were distributed amongst all the English naturalists, who regarded her work highly.

This interest helped to pull Georgiana out of illness and despair after the tragedy of her son's death. The little boy, almost two and always wandering, had had a bell hung about his waist to keep track of his movements. Despite constant supervision, he fell into a well and drowned. To her friend Captain Mangles she was able to let out some of her emotion:

> . . . *the fatal truth stole over me and Charlotte going up to the well,* she said: *Here's the Boy and pulled out that darling precious child, lifeless, his flaxen curls all dripping, his little countenance so placid he looked fast asleep, not dead. And we do not believe he was until minutes after. But the medical man was away and we did not know what to do. We tried every means of restoration but to no effect. And that lovely, healthy child, who had never known pain or sickness and had been all mirth and joyousness, was now a stiff corpse.*

During her long recovery period Georgiana was aided by her ramblings for new specimens and in the work of packing, drying and mounting seeds and flowers. The Molloys were also to move to the Vasse River, where Captain Molloy had taken up land and started to build a house. The thought of moving from the beautiful garden she had made was distressing.

Another daughter, Amelia, was born in June 1838 and as Georgiana was quite ill, it was fortunate the baby was healthy and happy. She described her to Captain Mangles and told him about the garden and how sad she would be to leave. She also asked if he could procure a garden rake for her, suitable to a lady's hand and not with formidable teeth which would spread destruction and annihilation everywhere.

The move was made in May 1839, upriver by whaleboat for the first part, then Georgiana and the baby on horseback and the girls riding donkeys. First sight of the new home must have disappointed her. It was on the bank of the river, but the Vasse was a placid trickle compared with the wildly beautiful Blackwood. There was no garden, nor was the house so attractive. However, it gave her a new interest and Georgiana set about creating a new home at the place they called Fairlawn.

Soon she had a real friend. John Bussell had been to England, married a young widow with three children and brought them back to the Bussell property, Cattle Chosen. Charlotte Bussell and Georgiana became close friends, using a boat to visit each other across the river before the bridge was built.

With a real friend at last, a piano of her own and a new garden to make, Georgiana was busy and happy. But after the birth of another daughter, Flora, she became very ill; just one more of the pioneer women for whom constant childbearing was a greater hazard than climate, lack of help, flood, fire or loneliness. Even the company of her sister, on a visit from England, did not help her regain strength. A severe haemorrhage left her desperately ill, but she did recover and wrote a delightful letter to Captain Mangles thanking him for seeds and a microscope for her, a telescope for Molloy and gifts for the children.

> *They will be quite delighted with the mouth organ. We are all passionately fond of music. I have a little organ or a sort of instrument like an organ and piano united. This the children often dance to and at dear Augusta I used to take it on the grass plot and play till late by moonlight, the beautiful broad waters of the Blackwood gliding by, the roar of the Bar, the wild scream of a flight of swans going over to the freshwater lake. The air is perfectly redolent with powerful garden scents. We used always to have tea outside.*

Collecting, exchanging letters, creating the garden all combined to help her recover and for three years she was reasonably well, entertaining official visitors in what one visitor thought an admirable manner. There was no servant, no glass in the windows, only a clay floor and thatched roof to the kitchen, but with Sabina's aid Georgiana gave hospitality which showed 'that genuine good breeding and deportment are not lost sight of among English migrants'.

Although it should have been obvious that she should have no more children, Georgiana became pregnant again. Her seventh child (and fifth living daughter) was born on 7 December 1842 and named Georgiana after her mother. It was a difficult birth and the doctor was drunk and inefficient.

Another doctor was brought the next day and seemed to help for a while, but recovery was only temporary. During the summer months Georgiana simply faded away, and she died on 8 April 1843, aged thirty-seven. She was buried in a field near the house, but her body and those of her two children buried at Augusta were later reburied under little St Mary's Church at Busselton, where Molloy and many Bussells lie.

The Captain lived for a further twenty-five years. Sabina, 11 when her mother died, became his youthful housekeeper. In 1848, when she was 17, her charms captured the heart of the visiting Archdeacon Matthew Hale, a widower with two daughters, 5 and 3 years old. They married the next year. When Molloy went to England for his first return visit, the younger sisters moved in with the Hale family for a while. Mary married Edmund du Cane and lived in England. Amelia looked after her ageing father until she married William Richardson Bunbury. Flora married William Brockman. Georgiana, whose fiancé was killed during an exploration trip to Broome, remained single.

Fairlawn, completed soon after Georgiana died, is still there on one side of the Vasse River, facing Cattle Chosen, the Bussell home, on the other.

The Bussell Family
From l. to r: Lennox, Mary, Fanny, Charles, William (the only one who remained in England), Mrs Bussell, John, Bessie, Alfred, Vernon.

WOMEN IN THE WEST II

The Busy Bussells

When Frances Louisa Yates married a young clergyman called William Marchant Bussell, her new surname was appropriate to her active, emphatic personality. She passed the bustle and energy on to most of her large family, but particularly to her three girls — Mary (Polly), Frances (Fanny) and Elizabeth (Bessie). These four English women who went to

Western Australia in the early 1830s were more than a match for their tough new country. They thrived on difficulties, coping at various times with fires, floods, loss of property and income, lack of servants, money, clothes.[1]

Small in stature and big in ability, the Bussell women were survivors. Their names jump out from the early days of Western Australia's history. At Busselton, some of them are still there, buried in St Mary's churchyard, but all of them are there in spirit and in the boxes and boxes of letters in the Battye Library in Perth.[2] They were incessant, unstoppable, voluminous letter-writers and as there were nine Bussell children (who adored each other and kept in continual touch), as well as many Bussell aunts, uncles and cousins in England, the yellowing sum of their correspondence is considerable.

The Reverend William Bussell died suddenly in 1820, leaving a widow of only 40 with six sons, three daughters and very little money. His title of 'perpetual curate' applied only to the position, not to the stipend, and his widow's regular income shrank to the sum of £8, rental from a field leased out by the year. Fortunately William Bussell had taken out an endowment policy of £500, payable at the age of 21, for each of his children. They also possessed wonderful friends and relatives, who collected £3000 and invested it to give the widow an income for life. For the next ten years the family lived in highly respectable, genteel poverty, though William (at the Royal College of Surgeons) and Lenox (a naval officer in 'the Med') at times behaved skittishly and rocked the financial boat. All the boys were well educated, each endowment sum, as it came due, being used to shift the next son along.

Rock-solid John Garret Bussell, the eldest son, mostly arranged his own education, at public school and Oxford, with scholarships. His ambition was to be ordained a clergyman. He was on the point of ordination when the Bishop persuaded him to wait until the next year. Meanwhile Charles, who had just left school, put to his brother the idea of emigrating to Australia. Letters received from friends in New South Wales persuaded the Bussells there could be a good life in the colonies, 'where £100 will go as far as £500 in England' and 'a single gentleman here with a little economy might keep his carriage on £150 per year'. Moreover, Captain James Stirling had recently called for families to colonise the Swan River area, promising 'land along fertile river valleys and a wonderful climate'. John met Captain John Molloy, who passed on more information about the Swan River settlement and told him that he and his wife would soon proceed there. The Bussell family's future was reshaped. Mrs Bussell was sure that in the new country it would be easier to stretch a penny into a pound; she asked John to forget his hopes of the Church and he agreed.

John Bussell (26), Charles (19), Alfred (15) and Vernon (13), with their servant Pearce and enough goods and chattels to earn a grant of 2257 hectares in the new country, sailed on the *Warrior* in October 1829. They travelled steerage, fortunate in having been showered with provisions by good friends, as they had to look after themselves. Living 'rough' on the ship was good training for the kind of life they would have in Australia. John learned to make puddings; Alfred supervised the daily sweetening of the fetid water.

They reached Fremantle in March 1830. The Molloys and the Turners had come on the same ship and were their neighbours on their first land grant at Augusta. The three families helped each other considerably, but the country was so heavily timbered that John looked for better land. He found it 20 kilometres up the Blackwood River, and called the place Adelphi, Greek for 'the brothers'.

By that time Fanny and Bessie had arrived with brother Lenox and the family retainer, Phoebe. Despite the fact that Phoebe slaved for them all for the rest of her life, the girls learned to work harder than they had believed it possible for 'ladies' to do and they performed all chores cheerfully and energetically, except for the laundry. They loathed that particular task, especially Fanny—the thought of it once reduced her to tears. Many years later they came to accept laundry, too, as part of the Australian way of life.

They came on the *Cygnet* in late 1832. The girls had a delightful journey. Despite limited money and limited wardrobes—many of their clothes seem to have been of the 'pre-loved' variety, given to them by their adored and wealthy cousin Capel Carter—they were 'belles'. Their letters describe some of the shipboard flirtations and festivities. Bessie:

> . . . one of the sailors was elevated with grog this afternoon and became most noisy, brandishing his sword about and challenging anyone on board who dared set up a claim to Miss Fanny whose every word she speaks falls like honey dew from her lips. I'll fight for her. I will have her. So you see, she makes conquests even here.

About another admirer, Fanny wrote:

> Mr and Mrs Harris (surgeon and agriculturist) are on board with family, including Mr Joseph Harris. I wish I could impress on people's minds that I have made up my mind to be an old maid. They have given me away in turn to every gentleman on board but they have now finally fixed on Mr Joseph Harris and every word and look is watched. He is in high dudgeon with me because last night he gave me a coconut ring. I was going to accept it but he intentionally broke it in halves and said I will keep this half while you keep that. Then he made me another and said 'wear it until death'. 'I will wear it because it is pretty' I said but I did not place it on my finger. It is a great nuisance and worries me. I hope he does not intend to like me. Certainly the pleasure of a conquest is lost on me.

Later Fanny wrote: 'I will be *harrissed* no more! Vous comprenez?' She must have given marching orders to this particular suitor.

The girls stayed in Perth and in Fremantle, waiting for a ship to take them to Augusta, or for one of the brothers to arrive. One of their hosts was the ship's captain, Captain McDermott. Fanny wrote:

> . . . after ploughing through the fields of sand we came at last to a spacious dwelling of 12 rooms, offices, stables, etc. The dinner table was nicely laid with great abundance of glass and plate and everything most comfortable. We were there for two days in which time we employed ourselves in making baby linen for an approaching Master or Miss McDermott after which Mr Browne [Colonial Secretary] was kind enough to invite us to his country seat at Perth.

Of this visit Bessie wrote: 'You must never stir here without two or three changes of linen, plenty of stockings for fleas abound and the sand soils your clothing sadly'. Later: 'I can assure you that it is a very mistaken idea that anything will do for the Swan. The ladies are always most nicely and lady-likely dressed.'

Eligible young ladies were rare and there was some quick competition for the hands of the Misses Bussell. Fanny:

> ... *you would smile to hear the reports circulated about us. Bessie especially has been given to everyone here almost. I have been appropriated to the Lieut. Governor, to Mr Lewis etc. But you are mistaken in thinking that anyone at all will do for the Swan. The gentlemen here are as particular as in England, indeed more so but you must not speculate about your errant damsels, it will do you no good. Society has not degenerated in the least and indeed, selectness and refinement are more prevalent than in England yet no one scruples to assist in the duties of the menage.*

Their ship had arrived in late January, but it was March before John Bussell could collect his sisters and be hugged and cried over by them.

> *Dearest John, looking so well, my mother, rather barbarous though quite poetical, in large canvas trousers made by his own hands, a broad leather belt, hair and beard both long, somewhat, and moustaches enough to give a bandit look.*

The girls were to stay at Augusta with Georgiana Molloy, who had borrowed a cottage for them. Only Charles Bussell was at the shack at Augusta now; the others were working on the Adelphi property, building rooms and working their land. Charles had a job as government storekeeper at £60 per year, which helped the finances considerably. Life was very hard for the Bussells in their first three years and they were pleased to know the girls could stay with the Molloys until the Adelphi place was ready.

Far from missing the refinements and comforts of the Swan River, the sisters settled happily to life in the bush ... 'it is here,' wrote Fanny, 'that one sees the magnificence of emigration. At the Swan, European comforts and luxuries have already robbed this life of all its warmth and grandeur.'

The next month Bessie went up to the Adelphi property while Fanny stayed behind to look after brother Charles. Later, after she too was at the new place, Fanny often went back to see her brother or Georgiana Molloy.

The brothers had constructed a main building about 4·27 metres square, with thatched roof and clay floor, glass windows (great luxury) and a carved jarrah fireplace with shelves and overmantel. It was well furnished with piano, bookshelves and books. There was an upstairs room for the sisters and six separate rooms had been built around the main one. They had fences, a garden, stock paddocks and growing wheat, all accomplished in two years of heavy labour. On the night of 5 November 1833, with only Bessie, Alfred and Lenox at home, the house caught fire. Bessie wrote a vivid account to Fanny at Augusta, despairing but humorous. The piano had been saved, along with many of the books, a chest of drawers, bedding and clothes which had been somehow pulled out as the fire spread. Silver, china and the precious glass windows were saved, but most of Bessie's clothes were not. Her frocks, bonnets and shoes—so hard to replace—had gone, but she rejoiced that she had managed to salvage one pair of stays!

John Bussell had been thinking of moving yet again, for this Blackwood River area was not quite so good as he had hoped. The catastrophe of the fire decided the issue and the final move was to a beautiful area on the Vasse River, now named Busselton. Until a new house could be built, some of the family moved back to the Augusta shack. Bessie wrote:

> *I left the dear Adelphi at about eight in the evening, accompanied by Phoebe and Emma (a fairly unsatisfactory servant girl), our pigs, poultry, cats, dogs, cockatoos and pigeons, Mr Green (a colonial doctor), John, Alfred, Lenox and Vernon for our crew and the two boats to tow, very deeply laden, so you can imagine we did not expect to make a very quick passage.*

They also took the piano with them and this was put in the Molloy's sitting room, so for a while Georgiana had the joy of being able to play music for herself and Sabina. It was one of the few benefits she received from the Bussells, warm and generous with each other but not noticeably so with others.

Being genteel poor for so long, though with many well-to-do relatives, had accustomed them to accepting handouts and hospitality as part of living. Georgiana Molloy thought they were mean. To a friend she wrote:

> This accident has obliged the Bussells to halt at Augusta before going to the Vasse where Molloy and they have taken their large grants. They are genteel nice people and that sort of thing—but terribly close-fisted which gives us the idea they belong to the Take All family as we have on several occasions been most liberal to them. Yet they are not ashamed of receiving everything and you will hardly believe they have made no return; nor have Molloy or myself ever broken their bread!

Except for William, the surgeon, who did not emigrate and died in England in 1835, the Bussell family was complete when Mrs Bussell and Mary arrived on the *James Pattison* in October 1834. The Governor (now *Sir* James Stirling) and his wife were on board, also a well-to-do Scotsman named Patrick Taylor who had very much enjoyed the company of Mary. The ship had called at Busselton, where mother and Mary (Polly) enjoyed an emotional reunion with the boys, all working on the new place, before going on to Fremantle where Bessie and Fanny were waiting. Soon they were all living together again in the new house that was now to be the centre of family life: Cattle Chosen, so called because a valuable cow called Yuleika, which had disappeared months before from Adelphi, had been found there with her calf.

Cattle Chosen still stands, close to the Vasse River, though not quite the same as it was. Part of the house had to be pulled down because of white-ant damage, but the original sitting-room wing still exists, family pictures on its walls. A descendant runs the property.

John Bussell, who had been engaged for years to his childhood sweetheart Sophia Hayward, orphan heiress of a West Indian tea planter, journeyed to England to claim his bride. Some time before, he had written to her advising that

> . . . *in domestic affairs my mother must be paramount in her own*

circle; in general affairs such as are not the province of women, as experience demanded, I might assume control.

Five years later, when John arrived, the notion of Mrs Bussell as 'commanding officer' still seemed ludicrous and unacceptable to Sophia, whose friends insisted moreover that John was just another fortune-hunter. She broke off the engagement. Humiliated, John took himself and his broken heart to Plymouth, to convalesce with an uncle and aunt.

Shortly afterwards he met Charlotte Cookworthy, a well-to-do young widow with three children, and three weeks later they became engaged. Charlotte had been a member of the Plymouth Brethren and leading members of the sect were guardians of her children. They did not approve of John, who refused to 'convert', and threatened not to let her have the children. Charlotte, a determined and thoroughly delightful woman, arranged to kidnap her own children. She married John and sailed for Australia on a ship which stopped briefly at Plymouth. The children were brought on board to say farewell, and sailed away with Charlotte.

She was a splendid wife to John, coping magnificently with her autocratic mother-in-law, with her sisters-in-law, with her own large family—three daughters by John—and with her ever-present brothers-in-law. She loved the boys, particularly Charles, who never married—though he had made a faint effort towards it. When John went to England, Charles had asked him to 'arrange matters' for him with a Miss Elgie, who did not succumb to this far from passionate approach.

A second catastrophe to befall the Bussells was the loss of Mrs Bussell's household goods and trunks of clothes when a ship was wrecked on its way up the coast. Bessie wrote: 'All of Polly's vanities have gone to a watery grave and as ours were burned you see that destinies decry that we shall not be a vain family'.

Mary was the first to marry and was wed in Fremantle to Patrick Taylor, whom she had met on the ship. Governor Stirling gave away the bride. Of Taylor, whom Mary loved passionately, Fanny had written: 'Full of integrity and independence, I should like him indeed for either of my sisters but he is a man whose name I cannot even connect with the name of love'. Nor could she ever conceive of calling him by his first name. Taylor somehow lost his capital in land deals and poor investments, and he and Mary lived a fairly rigorous life in a small white house close to the sea in Albany. It is now a museum, with many Bussell mementoes on show.

Bessie married Henry Ommanney, who came to the Swan in 1830, worked as Assistant Surveyor and met Bessie during a trip to the Vasse. Several years after their marriage they went to England and settled there.

There were many suitors for Fanny, all of whom she rejected — even the rich Mr Leake, who made a journey to Cattle Chosen to beg Mrs Bussell to help him persuade her, she declined. A letter to John in England:

> It would have been an alliance which offered me affluence and ease and every comfort which wealth could promise but I could not strike my colours and your little Fan is still free in hand and heart.

Until well into middle age she remained with her family at Cattle Chosen, looking after Lenox devotedly during his terrible bouts of delirium tremens. He had been an alcoholic for many years and died in 1845, a week after his mother's death.

Fanny finally became Mrs Sutherland, marrying a widower with two grown-up children in the early 1850s. After he died, she wrote:

> It is just four years since he and I became one in mind and spirit. Our attachment has been no common one and I look back upon a period of unvarying affection and indulgence. He has often told me he did not think I should long survive him and he rejoiced in the prospect of a speedy reunion.

It was many years before that happened. Fanny eventually returned to Cattle Chosen and lived there under John's hospitable roof until her own death on 7 July 1881, aged 74 years. Her headstone in the churchyard at Busselton says simply: 'Aunt Fanny who left us sorrowing'. On the back is her name: Frances Louisa Sutherland.

Surrounded by Bussells as she was for many, many years, there were moments when good-tempered, loving Charlotte sought a little emotional relief in letters to English cousins. Of Mary's husband, Mr Taylor:

> . . . not one particle of warmth, but an excellent husband and father and quite as anxious and fidgetty about his bairns as Mary herself and she is more so than anyone that I ever saw.

Of domestic matters:

> All the ladies had such dread of the wash tub we could not raise our voices against it (employing a new washerwoman who would charge the enormous price of 4s per dozen). Fanny burst into tears and could not describe her horror of it.

Charlotte and John cheerfully tackled the washing together and became 'quite expert'; as did Fanny, once she had learned about soaking and starching and rinsing.

The bond between each member of the family was close and lasting. Charlotte:

> I cannot help wishing you were here to see all that goes on and to love the dear boys as much as I do. It is so beautiful to see their love for each other. John looks at them in pride, face beaming and they look upon me as one of the most excellent on earth.

As indeed she was. But even Charlotte must have yearned to be alone sometimes with her John, and it is her kindly shade that seems still to sit in the high-ceilinged room. It was part of the first Cattle Chosen and still houses their armchairs, a private sanctuary for the two of them. Charlotte does not lie beside John in the cemetery of St Mary's at Busselton. After his death she went to England and died during a visit to France, but other Bussells and many Bussell descendants are there.

There is one more Bussell girl to be noted: Grace Bussell, Australia's own Grace Darling, a 19th-century heroine. She was the daughter of Alfred, who married Ellen Heppingstone and built Wallcliffe House, a beautiful house not far from the family at the Margaret River. It was Grace who, in 1876, rode her horse into a wild sea many times and with stockman Sam Isaacs rescued fifty people from the wrecked ship *Georgette*.

Rachel Henning

DAUGHTERS OF THE RECTORY

The parsonages and rectories of 19th-century England contained an ever-increasing complement of daughters trained to light domestic accomplishments and socially acceptable leisure activities. They were ladies *born* and would remain so in whatever extraordinary circumstances they encountered, knowing absolutely what was correct and what was not, who was and who would never be *quite* a lady, *quite* a gentleman. For the sons, who would rarely inherit wealth, a good education would ease the way into one of the professions or the Church; for the daughters the occupation of being a lady was preparation enough for marriage, motherhood and the perpetuation of family values.

Revering their fathers, adoring and cossetting their brothers, sometimes devoting a lifetime to family demands, the members of this 'lesser' sex were unsung achievers, finding within themselves marvels of adaptability and toughness, becoming pioneers and colonial matriarchs, transforming bush cottages into replicas of middle-class England.

The three Henning sisters who came to Australia in 1853 and 1854 were daughters of the rectory.[1] Their father, the Reverend Charles Wansborough Henning, the son of a well-to-do banker, had spent his childhood in a Dorset manor house which had been the family home since the 16th century. When his father's business failed, the young Charles, recently graduated from Cambridge, with no prospect now of further financial support, went into the Church. At 28, in 1825, he married Rachel Lydia Biddulph, daughter of the Reverend Thomas Tregenna Biddulph, MA.

Rachel Biddulph Henning was born in 1826, Henrietta (Etta) in 1827, Annie in 1830. Charles supplemented his sparse income from various curacies and by coaching students, until in 1831 the family moved to a much better living, the parsonage at Stogumber in Somerset, a roomy house with a beautiful garden. There were four more children: Amy, born in 1832, Edmund Biddulph, then Henry and Constance.

After Charles Henning died of tuberculosis in September 1840, his wife and the seven children lived with her father-in-law in Exeter, Devon. Several of Mrs Henning's brothers and sisters had died of tuberculosis and she herself had the symptoms. In 1841 the two youngest children died of scarlet fever. Biddulph (Edmund) recovered from the illness, but was afterwards considered to be delicate. Mrs Henning's only sister, Henrietta Pinchard, lived in Taunton and Rachel leased a house there to be close to her. With many cousins and loving older relatives, the young Hennings enjoyed family life in Taunton until their mother died in August 1845.

Rachel, 19 and now head of the family, was glad to have the

advice and support of Aunt Pinchard and of relatives and close friends: the Tuckers, the Hedgelands and the Slomans, all of whom had sons or daughters in New South Wales and whose lives would in future be closely connected.

Biddulph, idolised by all his sisters, was offered a job in a Manchester bank when he left school. The girls left the Taunton house and rented a place in Wimslow so Biddulph would be able to travel daily to Manchester by train (still a snorting, smoky novelty). Etta was married in Wimslow in August 1851 to a recently bereaved friend, the Reverend Thomas Boyce. The next year Biddulph suffered a lung haemorrhage and decided to emigrate to New South Wales, where the climate was warmer and where he had many friends.

None of the sisters enjoyed robust health. Amy and Rachel had had bouts of serious illness and Annie had a persistent cough. Annie decided to accompany Biddulph to Australia. The other two would follow; Amy had an 'understanding' with Fred Hedgeland, who was about to emigrate.

On 11 August 1853, Annie and Biddulph sailed for Sydney. The SS *Great Britain*, making her second voyage, was a fast and comfortable propellor-driven steamship, a pioneer of the new route to Australia: the 'great circle' route went much further south than before, but considerably shortened the voyage.

Annie kept a sea journal to send back home and recorded a reasonably pleasant trip.[2] The Hennings were not even comfortably off, but there seemed to be money enough for the right kind of things. The two travelled first-class, at a cost of 70 guineas each and, of course, sat at the captain's table. There were times when Annie found it boring, but she was one of the fortunate passengers not troubled by 'the aborigines', the bedbugs which were such a frequent topic of conversation that the mention of them over the breakfast table incurred the fine of a bottle of champagne.

Annie, then 23, intelligent and lively, interested in fashion and so always smartly dressed, enjoyed the conversation and companionship of some of the officers. She found the captain's stories and jokes most entertaining. On some nights there was dancing on deck, with quadrilles, the polka and country dances, and several of the male passengers were sometimes prevailed upon to provide an evening concert. Annie was always aware, as her sisters were, of class; she drew frequent distinctions between those who were or were not 'ladies' and 'gentlemen' and some who never would be *quite*! Few on board, she thought, were ladies in the *true sense* of the word.

By dressing for dinner in what she described as a 'low' dress, Annie set an example shortly followed by other ladies, some of whom busied themselves cutting down high necklines to low. She and Miss Smythe, who had passed the behaviour test, took walks on deck together and accepted the offer of Mr Gray, the First Officer, to teach them navigation. Annie enjoyed the lessons as much for the quietness of the officer's cabin as for the learning. She often found it very trying in the crowded saloon where gentleman sometimes played cards noisily all day.

Sea air suited Annie. Her journal reports that she and Miss Smythe walked every day around the deck, around and around, sometimes as much as four miles. Her health remained excellent, but two little girls from the same family and a tragic young bride of 19 died of bronchitis and were buried at sea.

By late September they were experiencing bad weather, snow and icicles. The rudder broke for the fourth time and various mishaps prevented them from making a record voyage in the hoped-for time of sixty-five days. They anchored on Sunday October 16 near Williamstown. It was extremely hot, and Annie did not go on shore until Wednesday, when a party landed at a beach and took an omnibus into Melbourne, about 3 kilometres away, for a sum of 2s 6d. Annie considered the town to be quite attractive and not at all foreign-looking. Next day she enjoyed the visit to the ship of Governor La Trobe ('a tall, grave-looking man') and his party for lunch.

They reached Sydney on a windy, cold afternoon nine days later and she found it to be very beautiful. In pouring rain the next day their friend Captain Tucker came to take Annie and Biddulph to his house. There were so many old friends living in Sydney that when they moved to their own rooms in Cleveland Street, the Hennings had a busy and happy time with picnics, parties and riding trips. Amy's fiancé, Fred

Hedgeland, came to see them and neither felt able to give her a good report of the young man, who seemed to have made some unfortunate friends. He had become a musician instead of taking up a clerical position, and seemed quite unreliable.

Biddulph had decided to become a farmer and Annie, a cheerful and adaptable young woman, was happy to go where he chose. After a visit to cousin Linden Biddulph, who was farming near Wollongong, he decided to rent Elladale Farm, near Appin, and the two of them journeyed there. It was the first of many farms or properties that Biddulph would manage or own. Both he and Annie immediately enjoyed the Australian lifestyle; his health improved, and they felt this would be their future country. They looked forward to being joined by Rachel and Amy, who were to leave England on the *Calcutta* on 4 August 1854, travelling with another cousin: Tregenna Biddulph had the family weakness in the lungs and had, with rare consideration, asked his fiancée Bella Badcock to release him from the engagement because of it. Later, the climate in the Shoalhaven district of New South Wales having proved to be the restorative he needed, he returned to marry his Bella and bring her back to Australia.

Amy also kept a sea journal[3] during the voyage and was as critical as her sisters always were of the deficiencies in character which barred men and women from real gentility. The captain of the *Calcutta* was one she had to put in this category. Rachel, whose letters to her family over a period of almost thirty years record a great change in her feelings towards Australia and in her own emotional development, had many complaints about her fellow passengers. She was fortunate in finding that their cabin companion, Miss Maunder, a pretty 18-year-old, was indeed a lady. Alas, among the first-class passengers there were few others 'in the real sense of the word'. She found the voyage fairly tiresome, but accepted it as one of the wearinesses of life.

Soon after their arrival in Sydney on 21 October 1854 and their joyous reunion with Annie and Biddulph, the two newcomers were taken to the Appin farm. In early December Fred Hedgeland visited them there and Amy, finding the same unsatisfactory changes in him as had the others, broke off the engagement. After a few months on the farm, during which time Amy, despite chronically poor health and eyesight, turned herself into an excellent cook and housekeeper, she visited their old friends, the Tuckers, in Sydney. Here she renewed her acquaintance with Tom Sloman, whom she had last seen at his parents' home in England. He proposed two weeks later, Amy accepted, and they were married at St Paul's Church of England in Redfern on 6 September 1855. They made the arduous journey over the dreadful Blue Mountains road to Bathurst, where he became a bank manager and Amy the devoted mother of nine children.

The farm at Appin, though shared with her brother and sisters, did not please Rachel. She was not as socially minded as Annie, who made frequent visits to friends and cousins in Sydney and the Shoalhaven district. Amy seemed to enjoy doing the cooking and Rachel played her part by walking to the little township to fetch letters, by gardening and by reading to Amy while she worked or drew. It was poor soil on the farm and Biddulph had decided to leave for a better location on Mount Bulli.

Rachel was homesick for England. She could not fit happily into the colonial atmosphere and when her brother-in-law, the Reverend Mr Boyce, invited her to return to live in his home, Danehill (invited, indeed, his *three* sisters-in-law if they so desired), she kept the offer in mind. After Amy's marriage, and knowing that Annie was so happy in Australia, Rachel returned to England in October. Writing to wish Annie a happy birthday in March 1856 she said that while Annie fully deserved to have a happy life she felt that she, herself, would not find this possible.

After almost five years in England Rachel, though she was devoted to her sister Etta and Mr Boyce, knew that she must make a new path for herself and longed to see Biddulph and her other sisters. In February 1861 she returned to Australia on the same ship that the first two Hennings had taken, the *Great Britain*, captained by the same John Gray who had given navigation lessons to Annie and Miss Smythe. It was a good voyage, sometimes lonely for her as she judged fellow passengers by their 'look' and did not pursue friendship if the required standard was not reached. The people at her table were not, she felt, a very aristocratic set; but, mellowed by experience, she decided it did not matter for two months.

With faster ships, England and Australia were now only two months apart and many travellers made the journey often. Mrs Ranken, an elderly Scots lady on board, had just made her fifth visit to England. She lived in Bathurst, where she had some married children, and Rachel was delighted to find she was aunt to the Miss Ranken who had made the return voyage to England with her, that she knew Mr Sloman well and had actually met Amy and Annie.

In 19th-century Australia there was a strong network of linked and very large families whose children married each other or married the children of their relatives. Annabella Boswell's aunt was Mrs Ranken, and the Innes and Ranken families were closely connected.

It was Mrs Ranken who was Rachel's travelling companion when she visited Amy in Bathurst soon after her return to Australia. In Sydney she was sorry to have missed Annie, who had been visiting the Tuckers there but had already left to join Biddulph on his station property Marlborough in Queensland, with Rockhampton its nearest port. Both had been in Sydney for two months and had enjoyed a busy social life. Charming, gay-spirited Annie, fashionably dressed always and a bright conversationalist, was sadly missed. She was so popular that she had been escorted to the steamer by 'nine gentlemen and three ladies'.

The first stage of the journey to Bathurst was made by train from Sydney to Parramatta, but from there on the road was still rutted, up and down gullies, with the long pull up Lapstone Hill in the Blue Mountains after a punt trip across the Nepean River from Penrith. Rachel and Mrs Ranken were travelling in the new Cobb and Co. coach (from which the gentlemen often had to descend in order to push the vehicle out of trouble).

In Bathurst (where she judged the climate to be more like England than Australia) Rachel enjoyed meeting her two little nieces and Amy's baby son. Having now made up her mind that she would only think of the pleasant things in Australia, her attitude towards the country began to change. She wrote long, long, uncomplaining letters to Etta in England, with news of Amy's family and news of Annie and Biddulph in Queensland. She gave the first mention of Mr George Hedgeland, who was working on the property with Biddulph. They had all met him in England and Annie had found him rather pleasant and gentlemanly, compared with some of the other station men.

The letters of Rachel Henning, an intelligent and observant woman who had a definite feeling for the right word, provide sharp glimpses of the contemporary scene. While she was in Bathurst there was intense activity on the nearby goldfields and she saw many of the Chinese diggers in Bathurst, describing them as exact replicas of the straw-hatted, pole-carrying figures on willow-pattern plates. She felt, too, that in the riots at Lambing Flat the Chinese had been badly treated by the other diggers.

She planned to join Biddulph and Annie as soon as possible, but he had taken up a second property out from Bowen and such a vast distance from Bathurst that Rachel now adopted the philosophy of living and enjoying each moment as it came and allowing the future to look after itself. She did some gardening for Amy and looked forward to making a garden up north and unpacking the English seeds still in her luggage in Sydney. The sisters visited old Mrs Ranken and were most impressed with her new sewing machine. Amy was 'wild to have one'. They could be obtained in Bathurst, but Rachel thought that £10 for such a machine was a good deal of money.[4]

In 1862 Rachel was in Sydney with Annie. They would sail for Rockhampton in mid-August to be met there by Biddulph, who would escort them about 560 kilometres to his new property, Exmoor. Books, crockery and furniture had been bought and many boxes and cases sent off to Port Denison (Bowen) for collection.

Rachel was 36 now. Her gradual transformation from reserved, aristocratic English spinster into practical, adaptable, inventive and industrious Australian began with the journey north from Rockhampton. Biddulph had brought horses down and he, Rachel and Annie would ride to the first station, Marlborough, before going on. The main luggage had been sent on to the 'camp', where an advance party (including Mr George Hedgeland) waited for them. The ladies crammed their awkward crinolines and dresses into a valise which their brother carried with him on his horse. Rachel's personal things went into a saddle bag, leaving the big bags to be carried by packhorses.

On the first day, after a 37 kilometre ride, the ladies spent the night at a station homestead. Rachel saw her first Aborigines and remained unshocked at their lack of clothing. The second night was her first experience of camping, and she loved it. On a grassy place on the bank of a creek, with a pintpot of tea in her hand, with beef and damper made by Mr Hedgeland, with horsebells for music, a fire blazing, a carpetbag for a pillow and a bed of blankets and rugs, Rachel's heart and spirit were changed for ever. The Australian bush enchanted her and she had discovered a new home country.

After another 24 kilometre ride they reached Marlborough, which Biddulph had greatly improved and was about to sell. Rachel, who had always adored her brother, found him now as good-tempered and easy as ever, looking well and handsome and having become a first-rate bushman. She also liked his right-hand man Mr Hedgeland, who intended to run some of his own sheep on the new station Exmoor. The sisters packed up household goods to go on the dray for the ten-day journey further north. They travelled on horseback or in springcart. It was an adventurous journey, with many mishaps that Rachel made light of or seemed to enjoy. They preferred camping out to station hospitality, rejoicing in the beauty of valleys, creeks and trees, enjoying the boiling of billies, spreading of blankets and saddlebags by a fire, pinning up riding habits and composing themselves for sleep. By the time they crossed the Burdekin River they were within Exmoor's boundaries. They boiled fresh-caught eels for supper and Rachel was sorry it was their last camp, writing to her sister in England about how perfectly well and fit she had felt ever since leaving Sydney.

The Exmoor house was long and low and comfortable, built

of wood slabs. A piece of ground had already been fenced and dug for Rachel's garden, which she would plant as soon as there was rain. She thought the country around was very beautiful, with hills, bush, river and creeks. Among the station staff was Mr Deighton Taylor, a well-educated Englishman. He was the sheep overseer and Rachel found him rather shy, but with a good sense of humour. He had a great deal of black hair which she thought would benefit from a good cutting.

Within two months she was totally absorbed in the station routine. She had encountered her first snake, had been for some wild rides chasing kangaroos, had learned to 'turn a hand to anything' as a good bushwoman should. Biddulph could shoe his own horses; Rachel made Devonshire cream and butter; Annie and Mr Hedgeland had become good friends 'and may perhaps be more'. Like most of the English gentlewomen who lived away from the colonial towns and cities, Rachel learned to do many unaccustomed chores. On Exmoor, after the washerwoman had departed her job was done by Biddy, one of the Aboriginal servants, but for a while Rachel and Annie washed collars and delicate stuff and did some of the ironing. Life was so easy and enjoyable for Rachel that she felt this could not be considered too great a task.[5]

Rachel loved animals, looked after the fowls and triumphantly reared one emu chick of three that had been brought in; she was the guardian of young lambs and described herself in letters as usually to be found walking about followed by a train of nine lambs and with a quartpot of milk in hand. She fed them three times a day and was a loving shepherdess.

Biddulph was continually expanding property and stock, and everyone on the station, including Rachel and Annie, soon became jacks-of-all-trades. The men's help was sought to sew a complete lining of fabric for walls and ceiling of a new sitting room, and Rachel noted that Mr Deighton Taylor was particularly adept. She very much enjoyed his company and with Annie and Mr Hedgeland they were a regular foursome for walks and rides.

Roses and chrysanthemums were growing in Rachel's garden and there was an excellent kitchen garden, too. They planted figs, oranges, bananas and pineapples and it was almost a self-supporting household with bream from the creek, wild limes for preserving, their own poultry, meat, vegetables and fruit. In the spring the wildflowers delighted Rachel during her bush walks and rides and she found that time was passing almost too quickly. It was beautiful country and she loved it.

After the shearing towards the end of December 1863, when Mr Taylor had a gang of eight shearers working, Rachel and Annie talked of making a trip to Sydney. It was a wet Christmas, but Annie, with some help from Mr Hedgeland, prepared a magnificent dinner: roast beef, pumpkin and okra for vegetables, two brace of wild duck shot by Mr Taylor, plum pudding, apple tart and mince pies and watermelon to finish. The Sydney trip was long delayed by Biddulph's absence and by station work. The ladies' best clothes had been packed and sent down and by May 1864 they were a little desperate for clothing. Rachel wrote that she was stitching sheepskin patches on her boots, that their dresses were shabby and their undergarments growing threadbare. Climate and weather she found quite perfect, and there were always lambs to accompany her on walks. She had a little black one which followed her like a puppy. By now Rachel had accepted the idea that she would remain in Australia. Life was so comfortable and so interesting. The station, once the furthest north, was now one of many and was always a centre for visitors travelling up or down.

The hint of more to come between Annie and George Hedgeland was correct. They became engaged and planned to marry in Sydney at the end of 1865. Rachel herself had news; she was embarrassed and quite reluctant to write to her sister Etta, fearing disapproval. She had been engaged to Deighton Taylor for six months before she told her. She was 39, several years older than he, and felt foolish but was obviously very much in love.

Deighton Taylor was among the most unusual of educated Englishmen who turned themselves into excellent Australian bushmen. He was the grandson of a clergyman and the son of a quite extraordinary woman, Mrs Janet Taylor, whose husband had been a naval officer and later opened an inn. After his death she established a school to prepare midshipmen for navigation and mathematics examinations. Her technical ability was considered remarkable. She published a nautical almanac and opened a shop for the manufacture and sale of nautical instruments. Her son Deighton had been destined for the church, but preferred to accompany ships down the Channel and adjust their instruments. He had also worked at the instrument trade and had studied violin for two years and, Rachel wrote to her sister Etta, 'all the family is wild about music'.

'He has a most curious collection of knowledge, knows a great deal about chemistry, metals and astronomy. He sings beautifully.' He was also to be a devoted husband and companion for Rachel.

Rachel left Exmoor to accompany Annie and Mr Hedgeland down to Sydney, where they were married on 24 January 1866. She was never to return to the place she had loved and which had influenced her so much. She and Deighton Taylor were married six weeks after her sister's wedding. It was a very happy marriage. Six years later, when she spent two weeks in Sydney on her own to attend the much-anticipated marriage of her adored Biddulph (then 38) to Emily Tucker, she wrote that she and Mr Taylor never cared to be separated.

The Taylors lived first at Bulahdelah, near the Myall River in New South Wales, then at Peach Trees, near Stroud. But most of their married life was spent at their small, much-loved property Springfield, near Wollongong, where Rachel had a beautiful garden and they lived a simple and contented life together. They enjoyed simple entertainments and pleasures; musical evenings (Mr Taylor, his wife considered, had a very fine singing voice), visits from friends and relatives. Rachel had no children, but Annie Hedgeland had one son who enjoyed visiting his aunt and there was always a selection from Amy's nine offspring to come for holidays. Rachel may not have regretted missing out on motherhood, for she had sometimes considered that her friends were overburdened with too frequent babies.

Biddulph and Emily lived in Sydney after their marriage. They had three children and Biddulph became a successful businessman. Amy was the first of the three sisters to die; aged 59, in Bathurst, in June 1891. In 1896 Rachel and Deighton, an asthma sufferer, left their farm to share a big house with the Hedgelands in Ryde, close to Biddulph. Both Rachel's and Annie's husbands died there and the sisters moved to Hunter's Hill. Here, when Emily died in 1902, Biddulph bought the large old mansion, Passy, and he and his sisters lived happily together as they had in Queensland so many years before. Rachel, always a garden lover, enjoyed working in the Passy gardens. She died there, aged 88, in 1914. Annie lived a few years longer and Biddulph, their 'delicate', adored younger brother, lived to be ninety-four.

Janet Templeton

THE LADIES BO-PEEP

Janet Templeton and Eliza Forlong came to Australia in 1831, both bringing sheep with them as a basis for future prosperity. They were sisters-in-law; they travelled on the same ship; they were both 45 years of age and their lives had been and would be closely connected. They probably disliked each other very much, though neither would have admitted it. One went to Tasmania, one to New South Wales; both died in Victoria and are buried there.

Eliza Forlong was considered a most *remarkable* woman. (She herself would have been in complete agreement, for she had a fair opinion of herself, of her husband and of her sons.) Many of the men she met, including Sir Thomas Brisbane and various other officials in England who were linked in some way to the new colony, were most impressed by Eliza, though some found her a little too forceful and 'unfeminine'. Two Tasmanian governors who encountered Eliza found her quite formidable: Colonel Arthur and Sir John Franklin, who stated that 'I like a woman to be womanly, a lady to be always ladylike'. During several extraordinary years, when Eliza was walking through Germany inspecting and choosing a flock of sheep to bring out to Australia, she certainly would not have fitted that picture.

The Forlong family, of aristocratic Huguenot background, had left France and settled first in Ireland and then in Scotland, where they pursued such respectable professions as the Church and the Law.[1] Janet Forlong, daughter of a minister, married Andrew Templeton, a successful Glasgow banker many years older than herself. Janet's brother John, a perpetually hopeful business man who seemed always to lose more money than he ever made, found his brother-in-law an excellent source of financial aid. To Eliza, his wife, it always seemed most unfair of life to bestow riches and comfort and a big mansion upon her undeserving in-laws while her brilliant John was so frequently put down by circumstances.

In 1826 the John Forlongs were living near Glasgow. They were always concerned about the health of their two sons, the only survivors of a family of five children, the others having died of consumption. Eliza was devoted to her boys, particularly so to the older son William, then 14, who was considered delicate. It was Eliza who first had the idea of going out to the new colony where, she had been told, the bracing climate had restored the health of many ailing Englishmen. She met Sir Thomas Brisbane, recently returned from being Governor of New South Wales, and heard from him that wool growing was now a most profitable occupation in the new colony. Eliza saw a new future. Sheep from Saxony were considered the best in Europe and the Forlongs were inspired to take their sons to Germany to learn the wool business thoroughly. Eliza would stay on with them, learn the language and buy a Saxon flock to take back to England and eventually to Australia.

This bold and original scheme succeeded triumphantly because of Eliza's determination and single-mindedness. She was capable of any effort for her boys. For the late 1820s, her achievement was extraordinary. A gentlewoman—a genuine English lady—she tramped the lanes and byways of rural Germany (and ventured into France), her skirt sometimes pinned up because of mud and rain, her cash sewn into her corset, selecting sheep for the family venture. And it was a 'family' venture; Andrew Templeton had provided the financial backing for it. Indeed, without his financial help none of this would have been possible. He was devoted to his wife and she was devoted to her brother, whom Templeton had helped many times before.

After the boys were settled and John Furlong had returned to England, Eliza, by now speaking German with reasonable fluency, went to Saxony. It was a sparsely settled province where some of the small towns were still walled and fortified and the inns were primitive. Few foreigners, and certainly no foreign *women*, went there. Eliza was often received with suspicion and was sometimes refused accommodation, so that she had to 'sleep out'.

Shepherd's crook in hand and accompanied by one of her sons, she walked through the country twice, testing for fineness of wool with a probe the first time, the second time choosing the sheep. When she had bought an animal she would put a locked collar with her seal on it around its neck, making sure of her stock. There may have been times when the redoubtable Eliza would have liked to act like a conventional female and cry on a strong male shoulder, but she carried on as she had begun, though there were some bad moments. In a letter to relatives she wrote, 'I was fearsome when I heard the chains of the drawbridge rattle down on coming to a fortified town lest our passports and receipts should not be accepted'.

During four years and on three separate journeys to Germany, Eliza tramped about 2400 kilometres. She bought 100 sheep on the first trip and walked them an extra 290 kilometres to the port of embarkation; then walked them again in

England, from Hull to Liverpool. She sold some of them at a good price and went back for more. Finally they had their flock.

William sailed first, bound for New South Wales, with letters of introduction to important people. Both his parents were sure that with his family background, his sheep and his knowledge of wool, wonderful things would happen for William, including an immediate and immense land grant. Eliza was almost convinced that her son would be doing the colony a favour by going there.

The admiration and general acclaim with which her Saxon adventurings were received gave Eliza enormous pleasure and helped ease her sadness at William's absence. Never one to underrate herself, she enjoyed the retelling of her journeying. It truly had been a fantastic thing for a woman in her forties, and a gentlewoman too, to accomplish. If some of the ladies thought Mrs Forlong's behaviour had been extremely odd, the gentlemen continued to congratulate her.

William, 18 and independent for the first time, enjoyed both his freedom and his journey. His ship went first to Tasmania and he arrived in Hobart in late October 1829. He met the Governor and most of the influential people, sold some of his sheep and applied for a land grant. He had decided to stay in Tasmania. He was sure that his uncle would provide the extra capital needed. His aunt Janet had a large family of her own but 'doted' on William, who knew it and knew that she would influence his uncle on his behalf.[2]

No more loans were forthcoming, however. Soon after William left, Templeton became ill. His health deteriorated rapidly and he died two months later, leaving Janet a widow with nine children, the youngest only a baby. Soon after the very large funeral, rumours were spreading that the Templeton estate would not 'cut up' as handsomely as generally believed. The lawyer broke the news to Janet that, owing to some strange 'peculations at the bank', her accustomed style of living must be reduced. It was bad news for the Forlongs, too. With nine children (Agnes, the eldest, was 14 and William only a baby), Janet would have nothing to spare. Their dreams of following their elder son to the colonies faded.

It was Janet Templeton who revived and fulfilled their dreams by making a quite extraordinary decision. She had been advised to sell the Templeton mansion in the best part of Glasgow, with its magnificent gardens and furnishings, and buy a smaller place. Instead she began to consider the colonies as the best future for her children. A realist, she accepted that none of her boys seemed brilliant enough for professional careers. Meanwhile Sir Thomas Brisbane enthused about the country, about the future for wool. And where else would you get so much land for so little?

Andrew Templeton had thoroughly investigated Australia's wool-growing possibilities, had found out about its climate and culture and had shared his knowledge with his wife. Janet also knew that a school for the sons of gentlemen would soon be started. She decided to charter a ship to transport her family and belongings to New South Wales. Her brother and his family were to be included. John and Eliza were commissioned to return to Saxony to select a new flock. Half of it would be theirs.

The Glasgow mansion was sold, the Forlongs brought back a flock of 130 pure merinos and John disposed of his business. It was a complicated and lengthy undertaking; their capital had shrunk greatly (and baby William was 2½) by the time the family party sailed on the *Czar*. On board were three of Janet's staff: indispensable and much-loved Kitty Terrie; the cook, Catherine McCormack; James Brown, overseer, with three shepherds under him. There were the Templeton children (Agnes, 16, Margaret, 14, Christina, 13, John 11, Marion, 10, Janet, 8, James, 6, Andrew, 4½ and William, 2½) and their belongings; John, Eliza and Andrew Forlong; furniture for both families, all the provisions for the journey; there were the sheep, six Clydesdale horses, fodder and hay, farm implements and assorted merchandise.

They arrived in Hobart on 12 February 1831. Janet had chartered the ship to go to Sydney but because William Forlong had changed his plan and stayed in Tasmania, his parents felt they must remain there and tried to persuade Janet to stay, too. John was sure that they should all be together but Janet, who had grown used to making her own decisions since her husband's death, felt that New South Wales, being so much larger, would be better. She sailed on with the family and her brother went with her, still believing he could persuade her to change her mind.

He returned to Tasmania alone. Janet presented her letters of introduction, took a house at Concord and later arranged for her eldest son John to appear before the Land Board to apply for land on her behalf (he was too young for a grant of his own). She felt she was managing her own affairs well and possibly enjoyed being free from the company of her sister-in-law, whose travel experiences had tended to cast her in the managerial role in any undertaking.

On a grant of 1012·5 hectares in the Goulburn district, Janet pastured her sheep. She called the property Kelburn, instead of the native Conchipmolong, and divided her time between there and Concord. She was delighted to be able to send the boys to the new Kings School at Parramatta. In 1835 she bought land at Parramatta and built the charming house Roseneath, which is still there. She disregarded the many long, long letters from her brother in Tasmania, urging her to settle there, pressing the claims of its beautiful and refreshing state of moral and religious superiority and the better class of society there. John Forlong was a compulsive letter writer and among the Forlong papers in the State Library in Hobart are volumes of his writings: memorials to the Governor, diatribes and accusations of unfair treatment.[3] Neither John nor William, and certainly never Eliza, could ever stop believing that they deserved the best of everything. The colonial authorities in London also tired of John's constant complaints and demands.

Roseneath was built on land which had been part of a grant made to Bligh by Governor King and later disallowed by Macquarie. In 1840 Bligh's heirs made a new claim, also disallowed. Janet Templeton was the registered owner and it was in the drawing room at Roseneath that Marion, her 16-year-old daughter, met her grown-up cousin William Forlong for the first time in years. She was dazzled by this man of the world and William was charmed by the gentle, dreamy and lovely girl so unlike his formidable mother. He proposed during a ball at Government House and was accepted. There was opposition from her older brother John, now 17, and her eldest sister Agnes, but Janet was delighted. John was now managing the sheep property very capably, but his aunt had always seen William as without equal among young men.

John and Eliza Forlong made a trip to London, sure that *personal* application for land and favours would be well received. There John caught a chill, which became pneumonia, and he died there in November 1834. Eliza, shocked, grieving and lonely, took up the Forlong cause and appealed to or visited colonial officials. She returned to Tasmania and devoted her considerable energies to helping William with their property Kenilworth, which was beautifully situated, with a view of the western tiers.

After their marriage in June 1837, William and Marion honeymooned in Sydney. When they sailed for Tasmania, Janet went with them, both to offer sympathy to her sister-in-law and to profit from William's advice on running a property. Both mother and aunt adored him and his new young wife did the same, reinforcing his own good opinion of himself.

When she returned to her own property, Janet found that all the landowners were set on pastoral expansion. There was news of fine new country, rich land and good rivers in the newly discovered Port Phillip area. Van Diemen's Land was overcrowded and New South Wales was already well opened up, so this new country was tempting, a grazier's heaven. Settlers from Tasmania were already there; the Docker family from New South Wales had overlanded, crossed the Murray River and taken up land. Some of their neighbours were on the move and John Templeton, 18, said he was going too. Land hunger was a contagious complaint. Port Phillip was *the* place. The second son James would accompany John. Seven years earlier, Janet Templeton had taken the tremendous decision to transport family and possessions to the new colony and she was happy with what she had accomplished. Now, at 52, she astounded family, friends and neighbours by announcing that she would go, too.

Along the road that would become the Hume Highway, the Templeton party received hospitality and useful first-hand information from such people as Hamilton Hume, the explorer.

Janet's health was excellent and her spirits high. When there was no friendly house to stay in, she slept in a tent. When they reached the Murray River and had to begin dismantling the drays to get them across, she went over on the back of her horse, Neptune.

Crossing creek after creek as they went further into the country that became Victoria, they met several former neighbours and, finding that the country was as lush as foretold, they decided to settle in the vicinity of the Ovens and Goulburn Rivers, calling the place Seven Creeks Run. William Forlong also went to Port Phillip that year, and eventually owned several properties there. There were boom years and a drought year, and labour problems when transportation of convicts finished. The lean times began and squatters, over-extended, lost stock and property.

Money was short for Janet, too. She had made marriage settlements for Marion and for her daughter Christina (who married William Fancourt Mitchell in Tasmania, where he was then Assistant Colonial Secretary). William Forlong had also asked his aunt for help. Everybody was in need of money. Janet mortgaged her property Kelburn. In 1843 she sold Seven Creeks Run and the stock went, too. She also had to sell Roseneath and was one of many people declared bankrupt. A sale notice advertised:

> At the residence of Mrs Janet Templeton, some costly household furnishings, four poster bedsteads and hangings, engravings and books, chairs, tables, chests of drawers, hand-painted dinner set, china, glass, etc.

'By misfortune, without any fraud or dishonesty on her part, became insolvent', was the official record of her plight, 'together with many others'. All her beautiful things had to go, but the death of her daughter Margaret just at that time was a far greater blow than selling the house.

Janet's other daughter, Christina Mitchell, came with her husband to Victoria and settled on a property called Barfold, near Kyneton. There were few neighbours and fewer comforts, but she laboured hard, with her mother's resilience and toughness of spirit. The Mitchells turned Barfold into a show property and eventually moved to Melbourne with their large family. He became a member of the Legislative Council, and was knighted.

William Forlong alternated between bankruptcy and periods of great prosperity (during one of which he bought his aunt's former property, Seven Creeks Run).[4] His wife Marion took the children to England on a visit and never returned. His younger brother Andrew went to America. Some of William's nine children did come back to Melbourne.[5] During his visits to England to see his family, Eliza Forlong enjoyed managing Seven Creeks Run. She died and was buried there in 1859. Her grave is there still, now in a memorial enclosure by a quiet road near Euroa.

Janet spent her last years in 'reduced circumstances', living in Melbourne with her eldest daughter, Agnes, who never married but ran a small school for boys in South Yarra. In January 1857, twenty-six years after she had arrived in Australia, Janet died, aged 70, 'cause of death dysentery'. She was buried in St Kilda Cemetery. Agnes was buried there, too.

Mary McConnel

MARY McCONNEL— QUEENSLAND PIONEER

On 31 December 1848 the ship *Chaseley* was ready to leave England, under charter to Dr John Dunmore Lang. He was the strong-minded Presbyterian parson who was responsible for bringing many hundreds of Scots workers and families to the colony of New South Wales. This ship was one of three which would take a carefully chosen and superior group of immigrants to settle and develop the little townships that were forming in the newly opened district of Moreton Bay, about 800 kilometres north of Sydney.

Mary McConnel, married only eight months earlier, when

she was just 18, was with her husband David in the ship's cabin class. She was apprehensive about the future and amazed at her own courage and independence in going against the wishes of her family in Edinburgh and her friends. They had all advised against it and Mary, a devoted daughter, had been desolated by the hurt she had done to her parents. Her decision had been taken only after deep thought and much earnest prayer for guidance. 'Surely I was helped,' she wrote later. 'My subsequent life, I think, proves that my Father had chosen this way for His child.'[1]

Mary was one of the earliest of the genuine ladies who battled with the Queensland bush. She wrote about her life there many, many years later. Intended for her children, her nephews and nieces, *Memories of Days Long Gone By by The Wife of an Australian Pioneer*, was published privately in 1908.

In 1847 young Mary McLeod had gone with her eldest brother John, a naval surgeon, to visit another brother who was a doctor in Yorkshire. She met there an interesting and handsome older man who had recently returned from several years of pioneering in Australia. They were married in April 1848 and left for Moreton Bay at the end of December. They would have gone earlier had not her family been so much against it, for David McConnel's brother was managing his property for him and he was needed to take over. Mary prayed, and went with him.

The McConnels were not immigrants, but settlers, and reasonably affluent. Loneliness and the lack of gentlewomen's company were to be great afflictions for Mary, but there was money to ease things domestically and the McConnel property, Cressbrook, had been formed some years previously.

There was some congenial company on board:

> ... a good number of nice people among the emigrants who had availed themselves of Dr Lang's arrangements with the British Government that on payment of £200 they should have land privileges on arrival in the colony.

The McConnels and their maid had a good cabin, with well-filled bookshelves, and two swinging candle lamps giving a fair light. There was a large bed which shut up into a sofa during the day, comfortable chairs, a table and a carpet.

The experienced bushman David McConnel had also taken on board two terrier dogs, the most useful accompaniment, as the passengers were much plagued by rats. One of the terriers was always out on loan, the other always in the cabin where it was constantly needed. 'When at meals I always sat with my heels under me, the only protection I could have at these times.' Sometimes Mary took supper in the cuddy at 10 p.m. with Mrs Hobbs, the doctor's mother, who partook at this hour of bread, cheese and porter. 'One night a large rat came to the table and went straight for the cheese when there was a tussle but the old lady came out victorious!'

Mary enjoyed the company of some of the other young married women, 'all of us full of wonderment about the far away land that was to be our home'. There were many children and she was one who started classes for them on weekdays and Sundays. Many years later, in a baker's shop in Brisbane, Mary was told by the woman serving her that she was one of the little girls 'you used to teach on the *Chaseley* and I have never forgotten it'.

They reached Moreton Bay, soon to be renamed Brisbane, on 1 May 1849 'and what a dreary waste it looked'. The McConnels, the maid and the two terriers went in the customs launch, upriver to the town, and saw 'no sign of house, nor hall, nor men white or black'. Mangrove swamps were the only vegetation, but at Mr Thornton's cottage on the jetty they saw two ladies using a spyglass to see who was in the boat. They heard later of the great excitement with which the ladies had cried: 'There are bonnets in the boat! Who can they be?'

Mails being infrequent, McConnel's brother John had left for Sydney to meet them there and for a while they stayed in his cottage. There had been no rain for months, but soon came downpours. As roads were non-existent and not even the Government Resident, Captain Wickham, had any kind of conveyance, transport was done by river. Mrs Wickham (a daughter of Hannibal Macarthur and Maria King)—'a very charming young woman who later proved a good friend to me'—made Mary welcome.

They lived for a while in a small cottage on Kangaroo Point where most of the furniture they had brought had to be kept in the sheds, but the Collard piano, a much-valued wedding present, was accommodated by closing one door of the sitting room, putting the piano against it and entering the room through the garden. McConnel had bought land at Toogoolawah (now Bulimba) and a house was built here of white freestone brought up in punts from the quarry some way up river. Some houses, an inn, a small store and butcher shop also appeared on Kangaroo Point.

Mary's first visit to Cressbrook, a sheep and cattle station taken up by McConnel from 1840 to 1842, was a formidable experience. It was 145 kilometres down river and as she could not ride, they travelled in a four-seater Albert phaeton they had brought out. Hannah the maid travelled behind, along with the smallest amount of luggage with which they could manage. It took them two days to cover 40 kilometres of rough bush road to Ipswich. They stayed the first night with Dr Simpson, first Commissioner of Crown Law in the Moreton Bay district; the next at an inn in Ipswich, after which:

> ... it was up and down the gullies, zig zag to avoid the trees. Finally we came to Wivenhoe with a private room but a good deal of conviviality going on then another day of travel to Cressbrook.

She found it a pretty cottage, comfortable but fairly bare, where everything possible had been done to make it a house for gentlefolk.

> We took our meals in the common dining room. What a tea equipage it was! a tin teapot that would have held at least 8 quarters and took two hands to lift. Master and men share alike and I often sat down with 14 men, most of the travellers arriving at sundown which is never later than 7 o'clock.

Mary, troubled by the drab bareness of the sitting room, transformed it into what must have been the most cheerful place in Queensland—though it may have resembled a particularly elegant bordello! In the storeroom she had found a roll of unbleached calico, and as her husband possessed *three dozen* crimson silk handkerchiefs, she took twelve of them and with Hannah's help cut them into strips, then got the carpenter to make seats for the chairs, with a good-sized box for the ottoman sofa and two little candle boxes for stools, all nicely stuffed. The white calico covers were bound with strips of crimson satin 'and I had a pretty room to sit in'. The door opened on to the garden:

> ... and the beautiful hills beyond it. The bunya tree was growing quite stately by the path but it was all very solitary in this vastness, terribly so. I believed that the Lord must have sent me to this new land for some practical purpose.

When they returned to the house at Toogoolawah it had been greatly extended. Mary divided a big room into two with the invaluable unbleached calico for curtains, using one half as bedroom and the other as living room. The storerooms were behind and rooms for servants above. When a new immigrant ship sent out by Dr Lang arrived, they had suitable servants to inhabit the rooms: a man and wife as cook and laundress—indoor servants, while Hannah was housemaid. As the hot weather increased, Mary found the mosquitoes intolerable and took refuge in their large bed 'safely tucked up inside the net curtains with some work, books and writing materials'.

Early in 1850 another immigrant ship arrived, and now they had an excellent gardener, James Johnston from Edinburgh, with a nice young wife and a small boy. The garden grew quickly and soon there were several hectares of ornamental grounds in front and at the sides of the house, with a large kitchen garden and fruit trees.

The McConnels were excellent, thoughtful and farseeing employers, ideal settlers.

> *My husband wished to have and encouraged the settlement of respectable families near to him. He must have bought a good deal of land and portions of this he sold to his work people on easy terms and they began to clear it and make their homes. My first baby was born and Mrs Johnston was nurse. No special nurses to be had in those early days. I had a good doctor and all went well.*

A chain of migration was strengthening.

The Johnston's old parents arrived, also a brother and his wife and a widowed sister, the brother later becoming school teacher in Ipswich for many years. Our gardener rose to own a sugar mill built on his own land and ultimately became a Member of Parliament. He was a very intelligent man, read much, and a grand type for this country.

More Scots emigrants came to settle and spread through the district. By the time Mary was an old lady she was writing in her memoirs that three generations of some families had worked with them. David McConnel had started a large herd of milking cows, tended by one of the migrants. Another migrant was a fine cabinet maker and made beautiful furniture for the house.

Population was increased and people were busy clearing, draining and ploughing and thus began a thriving district now called Bulimba, with my husband the centre of it.

The McConnels took Sunday-school classes for boys and girls and two Church of England ministers sometimes came from Brisbane to hold a service in the house. The river was still used for transport, and if the tide was right the family would take two boatloads to the town for Sunday morning service. Then David McConnel bought a strip of land on the north side, fenced it, made a road and built stables, a small house and a hut. The ferryman lived in the hut and the family conveyance could be left there.

'A good many people were Presbyterians, all doing well, and a committee was formed and a church seating about 200 built at Kangaroo Point.' In 1852 Mary was overjoyed when her younger, 'delicate' brother, Reverend Walter McLeod, came, 'for not one kent face had I seen before'.

The McConnel's first baby, Harry, was a lively and adventurous child. On one occasion the pineapple crop had been so successful that Mary decided to send 1 cwt (over 50 kg!) of pineapple jam to relatives in England and Scotland. The fruit was reduced to pulp, placed in large earthenware containers and sprinkled with sugar. That night Mary woke up at about

2 a.m. and was impelled (by the Lord, she always believed) to walk down into the nursery. There she found Harry in a fit,

> . . . face dark purple, foam round his mouth, eyes glazed, he rigid with cold. I took him in my arms, waked the nurse and called my husband. A kind friend and neighbour who had written lists of rules for a young mother for me had said NEVER BE WITHOUT HOT WATER and I adhered to the rule faithfully and so that our darling child was soon in a hot bath and became less rigid. I tried to give him an emetic but teeth were clenched until at last he brought up a great quantity of pineapple pulp! All day and not noticed Harry had been running back and fro and each time taking a handful of the pulp. Could I ever doubt the ever watchful eye of our Father in Christ our Lord for this deliverance?

After the birth of her second son, with 'the best and kindest of husbands' and her beloved brother's company, Mary felt happy in her new country. But she began to feel a hollowness inside one knee and the muscles stiffened. The doctor at first advised rubbing it for twenty minutes daily, but it grew worse and he suggested the climate at Cressbrook would be better for her health. They made the trying journey there, but the knee became worse and then gangrenous. Mary was desperately ill and the journey back to Brisbane, in rain, through country which was mostly swamps, was terrible. It took four days, during which time she had to be strapped in by ropes, and to get down a bank she and the two babies had to slide down through the mud.

Finally, when it was thought that Mary was dying, she said goodbye to her husband and children and prepared herself. Then David McConnel asked the help of an elderly German doctor. He put Mary on board a river steamer and took her to Dr Sachse. First Dr Sachse proposed amputation, but Mary refused and a treatment began of pouring liquid caustic soda down the leg where the fistula was. 'I did not feel it any more than if it had been water.' At last she experienced a tingling in the leg and began to recover. Finally she felt well enough to send for nurse and the children. The baby, seven months old, became sick

> . . . and my beautiful boy died in my arms. I tried not to fret but

accept my Father's will. Time wore by and I was allowed to use crutches. In about a year and a half I walked as well as I had ever done.

On Harry's fourth birthday and after five years in Australia, the family went to Sydney and then to Scotland, David McConnel feeling that the Queensland climate might have been wrong for his wife. There was a rapturous reunion with the family, who made much of Harry 'and did not feel inclined to realise he was an Australian!' On 11 August her third son was born. During the next seven years, spent in Scotland, England and on the continent, two sons and two daughters were born: 'my husband went once to Australia and while he was away my baby died, our fourth child, two months old which was a great grief to me'.

When David felt he must go back again to look after the property, Mary's doctor said her health was excellent and she returned in 1862. Shortly before this the Moreton Bay district had become a colony called Queensland, with Brisbane as its capital. The first Governor was Sir George Bowen. His Greek wife, a very beautiful woman, had been the Countess Diamantina Roma and left her name behind her in a town, a huge river and a railway station.

The McConnels, who had brought a governess, Miss Sargeant, out with them, set out for Cressbrook 'in a phaeton which carried them all, the luggage following in a waggon'. They camped out at Sandy Creek, some 24 kilometres from the property.

The dining room of the old house now became a schoolroom and Sunday-service room.

> *My husband had brought many people to the station — splitters, sawyers, carpenters, builders, bricklayers. Some of the men brought wives and families which gave me a fuller life. I went amongst them, saw to their huts and began a school for the children. Then we got a respectable teacher. We provided her rooms, food and firewood and £10 per year. The children paid 6d and 4d weekly. This was a few years before the state school was begun.*
>
> *Then we began a small library for the men, fitting up a room at the back of the cottage. I made it very comfortable with good cedar*

tables, pens, ink and paper, a good kerosene lamp and in winter, a fire.

Sandy Creek became the town of Esk. David McConnel provided land for a church and manse. Then a state school was established. There were also enough children on the property at Cressbrook for a provisional school.

Mary McConnel no longer found the bush dull or isolated. There were always friends staying and there was much activity on the property. She visited the school, held a weekly mothers' meeting and for three years, when they had eight South Sea Islanders ('mostly Christian') working at Cressbrook, she taught them lessons and scripture.

Harry married in 1877 and eventually managed the property when his parents moved to Witton Manor, 10 kilometres upriver from Brisbane.[2] They were often at Cressbrook, but the new place was headquarters and they both were deeply interested still in helping migrants settle. Mary was full of admiration for the wives who worked so hard helping husbands to use crosscut saws and to grub out roots, living in tents until the huts could be finished. She was worried about their children, however, so far from medical help in times of sickness and accidents. A springcart on rough roads made a hard journey to town, the doctors were busy and often parents could not afford the 10 shilling fee. Some of the children died. Mary saw it happen at the Bowen Hospital, as the general hospital was called; there was no room there for children and all the men's and women's wards were occupied.

> *I thought it was time to have a children's hospital and resolved that with God's help there should be one, in Brisbane. In all Australia there was only one and that in Melbourne, the capital of Victoria. I invited a large number of ladies and younger children to tea in the Witton grounds and told them of the suffering little ones. The response was wonderful.*

All young people in the colony were asked to help. Six months later, at the annual Agricultural Pastimes and Industries Exhibition in Brisbane, a collection of work from children everywhere was sold. The poet Brunton Stevens wrote a verse, 'For My Sake', and it was printed on leaflets which sold well.

The fruit of their labours was the Brisbane Children's Hospital. 'From the time of the hospital's opening on 11 March 1878 till to-day,' Mary wrote so many years later, 'it has prospered and it is now the largest in Australia and is continually being enlarged.' Few women can expect to leave behind them such a solid and enduring memorial as Mary McConnel did, and she concluded her book on a note of satisfaction that the project had grown so successfully.

> My children are acquainted with the subsequent years of my life and my pen is no longer needed to recall them. These memories are of the Old Times and they are at an end.

Mary died, aged 80, on 4 January 1910. One of her children, Mary McConnel Banks, wrote her own memories of her mother. She wrote of the happy domestic life at Cressbrook, of many visitors, croquet on the lawn, 'with the wide hoops and still wider crinolines of the players spread bravely on the grass'. Attending prayers and sermons read by her father, she herself delighted in being decked out in a crinoline 'which was extemely difficult to control when I knelt'. And there is a superb word portrait of the older Mary McConnel, a woman of strong character, controlled, capable, religious; perhaps a little humourless. On one occasion a party from the house went bathing in the river and one of the maids lost her footing in a deep pool. Anne, the laundress, cried in panic: 'I can't help you! I can't help you!'

> My mother leapt into the water, her crinoline making a great splash and called 'Anne, Anne, you foolish woman, stand up and hold my hand at once'. This Anne did, knees shaking under her while my mother went to the edge of the pool, holding out her other hand to the sinking girl . . . We watched, awe inspired . . . It seemed as if the end of all things had come when my mother, the ruler of the house, upholder of seemliness and order, was seen making her way through the river, a wide wake following her, her shady garden hat still on her head, her crinoline only half-submerged and moving up and down with each step forward.

It makes a memorable last glimpse of a courageous, inspiring, inventive and always *dignified* Queensland pioneer woman, Mary McConnel.

Harriet and Dominic Daly

HARRIET DALY OF DARWIN

'Blanket' was the name the Douglas family gave to tinned meat, and they grew very tired of it. 'Blanket, blanket, blanket . . . ironclad food from one month's end to another. Curry, hash, mince, stew, nothing disguises it.'[1] So Harriet, the eldest Douglas daughter wrote, many years after she had left the primitive settlement at the top of the Northern Territory which would become Darwin.

Portuguese navigators first saw the place in 1606, and about two and a half centuries later the explorer John McDouall Stuart finished a great trans-Australian journey there:

> ... on the bright and sandy shores washed by the warm and tranquil waters of the Indian Ocean I hoisted the Union Jack and took possession of the country on behalf of South Australia.

Captain Phillip Parker King had surveyed the coast in the *Mermaid* in 1818 and several attempts at establishing a settlement had been made before Captain Bloomfield Douglas was appointed Government Resident of the Northern Territory.[2] His adventurous family—wife, five daughters and two sons—accompanied him to the isolated and remote place where they would establish a home and introduce to it as many of the colonial niceties as they could.

They sailed from Adelaide in April 1870 in the schooner *Gulnare*. Nine Douglases, the maid Annie, a pet jackdaw, the captain's wife and baby and one other passenger, a police trooper on his way to join the Mounted Force in Port Darwin, crowded on to the small (204 tonnes) ship. Furniture and bulky luggage would follow on the barque *Bengal*. Harriet and her sister (whom she identifies only as 'N') were the eldest in the family; the youngest, Johnny, was two.

Their first port of call was Warrnambool, on the Victorian coast. It was fortunate that they spent several hours there, because they then caught only the end of a severe storm which nevertheless battered the little ship so badly that the captain took her straight on to Brisbane for repairs. N and Harriet were delighted to find they had arrived there just in time for race week and the Queen's birthday ball. Their best clothes were all in trunks on board the *Bengal*, but they bought suitable material, made evening dresses by hand and went to so many dinner parties, picnics, dances and boating parties that Harriet recalled the three weeks in Brisbane as amongst the happiest of her life.

When they sailed into Port Darwin, almost two months after leaving Adelaide, Harriet thought it superbly beautiful; 'perpetual summer but very lonely'. For a while the two older girls thought of the place as exile, 'too far from pomp and vanities of the wicked world', but both became very attached to it.

The settlement was called 'the Camp' and the Union Jack flying on Fort Hill was a familiar and welcome symbol of the

British Empire. Palmerston, as the town was named, was picturesque but primitive, a handful of log huts and tents. Members of the Laragiya tribe were close by. Huts in the main camp had neatly thatched roofs and at the far end the girls were delighted to see a stable well filled with horses, for they were both excellent riders. The police barracks was close by.

> *The quarters assigned to our use were two huts, not large enough for such a party but pleasantly set close to the sea and moreover, the best the place afforded. The huts were very rough and only by good management we fitted. The sleeping quarters were in one large hut divided by partitions, the places between them were plugged with paperbark and roof also was bark, floor of pressed mud mixed with gravel, limestone and sand and windows fitted with unbleached calico. The floor was a great trial for the edges of our clean dresses became soiled immediately. There was one sitting room joined to the hut by a covered way, a galvanised iron hut about 26 feet long with the luxury of a wooden floor, iron roof shaded by bark, but very hot.* [3]

They arranged the furniture as well as they could and began to feel more comfortable after a verandah had been added with awnings made from saplings and canvas. Comfortable chairs and a table were installed and the family spent most of their leisure time there.

There was always music in the Camp. Most of the men played a concertina, some of them were flautists, and regular musical evenings were held. N had a lovely soprano voice and when the Douglas piano arrived, 'All came to hear her'. Harriet, an enterprising young woman, had decided to have some lessons in piano tuning before leaving Adelaide and when, during the wet season, the piano inevitably gave trouble, with the help of the blacksmith she kept the instrument in reasonable repair. 'However', she wrote, 'a harmonium sent up for a future church suffered severely from bronchial attacks as well as from consumption brought on by white ants.'

The settlement had sixty people, a large government store, a Survey and Lands Office, a Public Works Department, a Police Force and a Medical Officer, Dr Miller—'one of the dearest friends we ever made'. Much of their food was, at first, tinned. They accepted cheerfully the challenge of turning it into interesting meals, but the lack of fresh meat was keenly felt. Bread was baked by a government cook and Mrs Douglas became expert at producing batches of scones and cakes from a camp oven. There was a great deal of visiting in the evening, the men neat in fresh white shirts and what Harriet called 'the prettiest ties'. Members of the Police Force, she wrote,

> . . . dressed very like an Indian Light Cavalry Regiment, Royal Blue Garibaldi shaped jumper and facings of black quilted satin, with black and silver on the cuffs, trousers of dark blue cloth with silver stripes down one side and silver-edged cap. They were very superior and well educated and refined.

The maid Annie, whose flirtations had very much divided the ship's crew on the voyage from Adelaide, 'cut a swathe in the Camp but married one of the best fellows in the Government employ'.

Horse riding was a great pleasure and they often rode to Fanny Bay to gallop the horses across the fine white sand. They were always accompanied by a military orderly and usually left home early, picnicked for lunch at a favourite river place and rode home in the evening, to avoid the heat. 'Except for leeches and a special cruel form of mosquito', Harriet wrote, these days were spent in a tropical paradise. There were usually gentlemen in the party who went off to shoot wild ducks while the two girls looked for ferns and flowers. They also practised revolver shooting, with N always winning the first prize.

Picnic races were held at Fanny Bay, with tents pitched for dinner and a seine net out for fresh fish to take home. There was always an escort of Laragiya natives, with whom the Douglas family had made friends. They were pleased to have some of the women come to the house to help with washing. N and Harriet did the actual washing while the black assistants rinsed, emptied tubs, brought fresh supplies of water and always made a game of hanging out the clothes. Harriet was sorry for the women, whom she felt were very badly and selfishly treated by their men.

They enjoyed the basic lifestyle, and the Sundays with sermons read by the doctor and N leading the choir in lively singing, but the isolation was immense. They all yearned for mail, for news and parcels from civilised places, and the girls often rode to the coast to search the horizon for a sail. After three months the *Gulnare* came. Sacks of letters and newspapers arrived for them and that night they sat up very late, reading.

'Can it be credited,' Harriet wrote, 'that the whole Franco-Prussian war had been fought and the deadly struggle over before we had even heard of the prospect of a war at all?'

The Overland Telegraph Line was under construction.[4] Adelaide would be linked with Darwin, and from Darwin Australia would be linked to the rest of the world. Harriet played a minor role in the miracle. At the ceremonial planting of the first pole on 15 September 1870, Harriet, in a full, ground-sweeping white dress and a fetching white platter hat, took up the mallet and rammed the earth firmly down around the pole.

Life became more comfortable for the Douglases the next year when an official residency was built, but construction was a long and troublesome process; much more difficult than for Robinson Crusoe, in Harriet's view, for they had no well-found ship conveniently wrecked on the shores. Stone was the only available building material and eventually a bungalow-style house was erected, a long centre room of stone with bedrooms and bathrooms and pantries made of wood opening on either side. A lime kiln was built to burn coral and, as ironbark was useless for sawing, cypress pine was cut in their own sawpit. The timber in the flat roof warped, so it was overlaid with concrete and at night this became a favourite sitting-out place, reached by a ladder from the ground.

Life was becoming quite civilised. Mrs Douglas had a poultry yard with ducks, geese, fowls and pigeons which gave variety to the menu. All the children had pets, including a monkey, and Harriet had a parrot which was a tea drinker and preferred its early morning tea very hot. Harriet was enjoying life. She found the climate suited her and in their first seventeen months there had been no case of fever 'though we were all exposed to wind and weather and the sun'. The wet season was trying. She liked it for its coolness, but not for its destructive properties—'boots, books and other belongings covered in mould'.

> All the flour has to be sifted because of mildew and weevils, also oatmeal. *Preserved potatoes are tasteless, dried and granulated, had to be spread out on a sieve or cloth and examined most carefully before being soaked and boiled. Hundreds of cockroaches devoured our sugar, made meals of our boots, the covers of our books and any stray piece of flannel that comes their way. White ants devour clothing, paper, the wooden telegraph poles and* literary ants—*as in the Bible*—read, marked, learned and digested *the greater part of our books.*

They had brought plants with them from the Brisbane Botanical Gardens and these began to flourish and enriched the diet. In the garden soon were mangoes, bananas, melons, pumpkins, cucumbers and pineapples. Tomatoes, too, grew so well that

> ... *we were able to add them to our daily dish of 'blanket' and grumbles were fewer. Rosellas we grow plentifully and my mother who was very clever at home-brewed ginger beer managed to invent rosella syrup, one of the most refreshing of beverages. I had great success with cockles*—*I stewed them, made them into soup and crowned my efforts by scalloping them, deceiving everyone into the belief they were oysters.*

It was nine months before the second boat came with mail, and another six before the third arrived. The girls' clothes had become very worn and shabby, but they had discovered the virtues of unbleached calico and made dresses for themselves and the younger ones, trimming 'the unlovely surfaces with finely wrought designs in blue and pink cotton'.

Unattached young ladies were as rare in Darwin as a snowflake on a tree and there was a profusion of beaux for the two girls. Elegantly clad police officers, surveyors and government officials were constant callers, but by the middle of 1871 a choice had been made.

Dominick Daniel (Dan) Daly had gone to South Australia as ADC to his uncle the Governor, Sir Dominick Daly. When the latter died, Dan Daly, who had been trained as a surveyor, joined the government in that capacity. He went north with

G. W. Goyder's party and enjoyed his part in surveying 202 500 hectares of new country in 1869. A competent musician and actor, he enlivened the tedium of camp life by playing the flageolet, singing, acting and declaiming his own verse drama compositions.

Daly was a good mixer and relished hard work and outdoor life. He was one of the few who seemed actually to enjoy living in the tropics. In a letter to an Adelaide friend, he wrote:

> *I find I can stand the climate better than most but I am in very good health. It is hard work under a very hot sun but I would not mind the work if the sandflies would let me sleep at night. The mosquitoes cannot get in but sandflies get through the muslin and sometimes we are without sleep two or three nights running. We are working as hard as we can to get the work done and double our pay if possible and hope to see you all again at Christmas.*

When he returned from Adelaide, the Douglas family had just arrived. Very soon after that he wrote to his sister, also called Harriet: 'There are two Miss Douglases, very pretty and accomplished and I fear I am in a fair way of marrying one if not the other'.[5]

'The one' was to be Harriet. ('The other' would marry the superintendent of the cable station, Mr J. Enston Squier.) Harriet went back to Adelaide in September 1871 to be married to Dominick Daly and they lived for ten months at Naracoorte, 'where life was very pleasant with coursing, kangaroo hunts, many many visitors and balls'.

Meanwhile, the two ends of the Overland Telegraph Line had been joined and on 22 August 1872 a message was transmitted directly from Adelaide to Darwin. When she heard of this, Harriet recalled the planting ceremony and was glad to have been part of it.

As the Dalys both liked the Northern Territory, they decided to return. They sailed in September 1872 in the *Omeo*, which was joined in Melbourne by many diggers off to find fortune in the new goldfields in Queensland and the Territory. In Darwin they found many changes.

> *The Overland Telegraph and Cable Company had built substantial sandstone dwellings near the Government Residence, there were log*

> huts and many ships were in harbour. Parties of diggers left each day for the goldfields 110 miles away. Supplies were very expensive, flour £20 per ton and even 'blanket' was outrageously high in price.

As the place grew, more shops opened and some drinking saloons, too. In this previously healthy place sicknesses began to occur and malaria spread through the camps. 'Many never got to the goldfields for when they grew better they took ship back.'

Harriet had a baby daughter who was as adaptable and even-tempered as her mother.

> *The climate seemed to suit her capitally and she throve apace though with little conventional nursing. Her earlier days were spent over at N's rooms in the cable quarters. We had a sort of large dish cover made and covered the frame with mosquito net. It fitted over baby's paraphernalia of mats and pillows and as she grew old enough to sit up and take an interest in people and things she was brought into the laundry in a nice clean American flour barrel in which she played for hours while I washed and ironed. Her young uncle, now four, made a great pet of his niece.*

Daly sailed for Adelaide to bring back goldfields machinery, which he thought would sell well. It was a terrible journey. The drunken captain grounded the ship in the Gulf of Carpentaria and it was Daly who took charge and navigated through the Torres Strait. When he returned he brought with him a prefabricated house, but the goldfields had not proved as rich as had been hoped, so they sold the house and furniture and left for Adelaide. They sailed on a very small ship (82 tonnes) crowded with sixty miners going back from Darwin, as well as Harriet, Dominick and the baby and a Timor monkey called Jane which kept the baby amused, shared toys and played with her. The diggers also made a pet of the child and often sang her to sleep.

Harriet never went back to the Territory, though she remembered it always with affection. When her husband went to North Borneo with a British company, Harriet was able to indulge her enjoyment of travel. Later they lived in London, where she published her book and also wrote a regular column of news from abroad for the *Sydney Morning Herald*. Versatile Harriet Daly was one of our first female overseas correspondents.

REFERENCE NOTES

Abbreviations
ADB	Australian Dictionary of Biography
AE	Australian Encyclopaedia
A&R	Angus & Robertson, publishers
HRNSW	Historical Records of New South Wales
LTL	La Trobe Library (Melbourne)
ML	Mitchell Library (Sydney)
MUP	Melbourne University Press
OUP	Oxford University Press
RAHS	Royal Australian Historical Society
Tas. Arch.	Tasmanian Archives Office
WAHS	Western Australian Historical Society
WAA	Western Australian Archives (Battye Library, Perth)
SL	State Library category

Marriage — Colonial Style

1 Journal of Arthur Bowes Smyth, Surgeon on *Lady Penrhyn* 1787–88. Facsimile, Australian Documents Library Ltd, 1979.
2 ibid.
3 Watkin Tench, *A Narrative of the Expedition to Botany Bay. A Complete Account of the Settlement at Port Jackson 1788–1791 with annotations by L. F. Fitzhardinge* (RAHS in association with Library of Australian History. A&R, 1961).
4 *Journal and Letters of Ralph Clark* (1st edn, 1787), Australian Documents Library with Library of Australian History, 1981.
5 Journal Arthur Bowes Smyth.
6 John Cobley, *Crimes of the First Fleet Convicts*, A&R, 1970.
7 Norwich (England) Library Archives, Excerpts from *Norfolk Chronicle*; Folk opera *The Transports* (Peter Bellamy); Don Chapman, *1788 — People of the First Fleet*, Cassell, 1981.

8   C. H. Currie, *The Transportation, Escape and Pardoning of Mary Bryant*, A & R, 1963; Louis Becke and Walter Jeffrey, *A First Fleet Family*, T. Fisher Unwin, London, 1896.

Esther and Jane
1   G. J. F. Bergman, *Journal of Proceedings of the Australian Jewish Historical Society*, vol. 6, part 2, Sept 1966; J. S. Levi & G. J. F. Bergman, *Australian Genesis*, Rigby, 1974; *ADB*.
2   *ADB*.
3   HRNSW; Helen Heney, *Australia's Founding Mothers*, Nelson, 1978; Mrs King's Diary, King Papers, ML, Chapman Papers (ML).
4   *ADB*.

The Captain's Wife
1   John Nicol, *The Life and Adventures of a Mariner*, Blackwood & Eden, 1822.
2   ibid.
3   S. M. Onslow, *The Macarthurs of Camden* (1st edn, 1914), Rigby with John Currey O'Neill, 1973 (many letters of Elizabeth Macarthur); M. Barnard Eldershaw, *The Happy Pioneer* (*A Peaceful Army*, Sesquicentenary publication 1938).
4   Hazel King, *Elizabeth Macarthur and her World*, Sydney University Press, 1980.
5   Onslow, op. cit.
6   *Elizabeth Farm Parramatta, A History and Guide*, Historic Houses Trust, 1984.

Anna Josepha — First Lady
1   The King Papers: Mrs King's *Speedy* Journal, 1799, and *Buffalo* Diary, 1807, ML.
2   ibid.
3   Mary Ann Parker: Voyage around the World in the *Gorgon* man of war (1795, London) and Chapman papers, ML.
4   Marnie Bassett, *The Governor's Lady*, Melbourne

University Press, 1940; Journal of Philip Gidley King, Australian Documents Library, 1980.

Girl on a Horse — Mary Reibey
1. Dymphna Cusack, *The Peaceful Army*, 1938; *Mary Reibey and her Times*, Women's Executive Committee and Advisory Council of Australia's 150th Anniversary Celebrations, 1938.
2. *Sydney Gazette*, June 1829.
3. Diary and Journal of Mary Reibey 1820–21, ML; G. B. Barton, *Evening News*, 1898, Extracts from diary. (Newspaper file, ML).
4. Indenture of Convicts, *Royal Admiral*, 1792, ML.
5. Nance Irvine, *Mary Reibey — Mollie Incognita*, Library of Australian History, 1982.
6. Entally House (Tasmania), tourist book. (Scenery Preservation Board, Tas., 1956.)
7. *Sydney Gazette*, July 1811, ML.
8. Lady Jane Franklin to her sister Mary Simpkinson, 22 February 1838.

'Lik a Ladey'
1. Catchpole Papers 1797–1811, ms. 1116, ms. 4211, ML.
2. Rev. Richard Cobbold, *The History of Margaret Catchpole — a Suffolk Girl*, London, 1846. (No pub. date on my 1st edn.)
3. Nance Donkin, *Margaret Catchpole* (Australians in History), Collins, 1974.
4. Records of St Peter's Church, Richmond, NSW.

Letters from Women
1. HRNSW, vol. 3.
2. HRNSW, vol. 2.
3. ibid.
4. Geoffrey Chapman Ingleton, *True Patriots All*, A & R, 1952; collection of broadsheets on convict experiences, including Lydia Esden and the *Janus*.
5. Library of Tasmania Archives.
6. HRNSW.

A Woman of Letters
1 Louisa Anne Meredith, *Notes and Sketches of New South Wales During a Residence in that Colony from 1839 to 1844* (1st edn 1844), Ure Smith, in association with the National Trust, 1973.
2 ibid.
3 ibid.
4 Louisa Anne Meredith, *My Home in Tasmania*, 1853, LTL.
5 *ADB*.

The Elegant Misses Macleay
1 Letter Journals of Fanny Macleay, Macarthur Papers, ML; two vols.
2 *ADB*.
3 Letter Journals of Fanny Macleay.
4 Morton Herman (ed.), *Annabella Boswell's Journal* (with introduction about Lake Innes House), A & R, 1965.
5 ibid.
6 *Historic Homesteads of Australia*, National Trust, 1969. (Brownlow Hill chapter, text Rachel Roxburgh.)
7 Clive Lucas, *Elizabeth Bay House Restored*. (Booklet reproduced from *Art and Australia*, vol. 16, no. 1, Sept 1978).

A Passionate Australian: Annabella Boswell
1 Annabella Boswell, *Some Early Recollections* and *Some Australian Blacks*, ML; Boswell memorabilia, Folk Museum, Port Macquarie.
2 Boswell, op. cit.
3 ibid.
4 *Annabella Boswell's Journal*, op. cit. (ch. 9).
5 ibid.

A Five-pound Future
1 Committee for Female Emigration to Australia, 1834 (posters).
2 ibid.

3   Violet Maxwell, *Wooden Hookers*, A & R, 1940 (stories of the old wooden ships used for female emigration); LTL.
4   Sydney merchant Edward Jones in a letter to Messrs Donaldson, Wilkinson & Co., London, 1834.
5   Henry Melville, *History of the Island of Van Diemen's Land 1824–35*, (1st edn, London, 1835), Libraries Board of South Australia, 1967.
6   Michael Cannon, *Who's Master, Who's Man*, Curry O'Neill.
7   Margaret Kiddle, *Caroline Chisholm*, MUP, 1950.
8   J. B. Were, *Diary on the William Metcalfe 1839*, J. B. Were & Son, Melbourne, 1964.

Lady Jane — An Independent Spirit
1   F. Woodward, *Portrait of Jane*, London, 1951; also *ADB*.
2   Kathleen Fitzpatrick, *Sir John Franklin in Tasmania*, MUP, 1949.
3   Lady Jane Franklin's Journals, copies of papers held by Scott Polar Research Institute 1837–43, Tas. Arch.
4   Fitzpatrick, op. cit.
5   ibid.
6   Lady Jane Franklin's Letters and Journals, Tas. Arch.

Women on the Goldfields
1   Pennyweight Flat Children's Cemetery, Castlemaine, Vic.
2   *A Lady's Visit to the Gold Diggings in Australia 1851–52. Written on the spot by Mrs Charles Clacy* (1st edn, 1853), Lansdowne, 1963.
3   *Geelong Advertiser*, 17 September 1851.
4   ibid., October 1851.
5   Pictures of goldfields life by S. T. Gill, LTL.
6   *A Lady's Visit to the Gold Diggings in Australia*.
7   ibid.
8   Michael Cannon, *Lola Montez: The Tragic Story of a 'Liberated Woman'*, Heritage, Melbourne, 1973; Margaret Nicholas, *The World's Wickedest Women*, Octopus Books, 1984.

9   William Howitt, *Land, Labour and Gold* (1855), Two Years in Victoria.
10 Mrs Buntine in Gippsland, ms. 8072, box 64 3110(d) LTL.

Women in the West I
1   WAA.
2   By C. H. Hemphill, East India Chambers, Leadenhall Street, in response to a Colonial Office circular in April 1829 advising of intention to form a settlement in Western Australia.
3   J. S. Battye, Western Australia, (London) 1924.
4   Georgiana Molloy, 1833 (WAHS, 79).
5   Alexandra Hasluck, *Portrait with Background*, OUP, 1955.
6   ibid.
7   Bussell Papers—letters and diaries of the Bussell family, including Fanny Bussell's Diary 1832–33, Battye Library (WAA 139), five boxes.
8   ibid.
9   Hasluck, op. cit.
10 E. O. G. Shann, *Cattle Chosen*, OUP, London, 1926; facs. reprint, University WA Press, 1978; pictures and memorabilia, Historical Museum, Augusta WA.

Women in the West II
1   Shann, *Cattle Chosen*, op. cit.
2   Bussell Papers (WAA 139), Battye Library, Perth; author's visit to Cattle Chosen, Busselton, WA.

Daughters of the Rectory
1   *The Letters of Rachel Henning, with Forty Pen Drawings by Norman Lindsay*, Bulletin Newspaper Co. Pty Ltd, Sydney, 1952 (many subsequent editions).
2   Joan Thomas (ed.), *The Sea Journals of Annie and Amy Henning*, Halstead Press, Sydney, with John Ferguson, 1984.
3   ibid.
4   *Letters of Rachel Henning*, op. cit.
5   ibid.

The Ladies Bo-peep
1　Nancy Adams, *Saxon Sheep*, F. W. Cheshire, 1961.
2　ibid.
3　Forlong Letters and Memorials, State Library, Tasmania; ML.
4　Launching of a Dream: Seven Creeks Run, Euroa, promotional paper, produced Seven Creeks Estate, 1982.
5　Howitt, *Land, Labour, and Gold*, op. cit. (ch. 13), vol. 1, pp. 279-70.

Mary McConnel — Queensland Pioneer
1　Mary McConnel, *Memories of Days Long Gone By by the Wife of an Australian Pioneer*, 1908; LTL (privately published).
2　National Trust *Historic Homesteads of Australia* — Cressbrook, Toogoolawah, text Sir Raphael Cilento.
3　Mary McConnel Banks, *Pioneering Days in Queensland*, 1931. Photostat pictures and material supplied by Oxley Librarian, Brisbane; Judith McConnel (Mrs A. Biggs), 'I Even Had a Sunday Doll', *Women's Weekly*, Nov. 1971.

Harriet Daly of Darwin
1　Harriet Daly, *Digging, Squatting and Pioneering*, London, 1887.
2　Darwin's history, *AE;* C. McKnight (ed.), *The Farthest Shore*, MUP, 1969.
3　Daly, op. cit.
4　Peter Taylor, *The Overland Telegraph Line*, Telecom; photostats from Archives collection, SA State Library.
5　Letter from Dominick Daly.

Bibliography

ADAMS, Nancy. *Saxon sheep*. Cheshire, 1961.
AUSTRALIAN Council National Trusts. *Historic homesteads of Australia*. Cassell, 1969.
BANKS, Mary McLeod. *Pioneering Life in Queensland*. London, 1931.
BARNARD, Marjorie. *Macquarie's world*. Melbourne: Melbourne University Press, 1947.
BARNARD, Eldershaw. *The life and times of Captain John Piper*. Sydney: Ure Smith in association with the National Trust, 1973.
BASSETT, Marnie. *The Governor's lady Mrs Philip Gidley King*. London: Oxford University Press, 1940.
BATESON, Charles. *The convict ships 1787–1866*. Glasgow: Brown, Son & Ferguson, 1959.
BEATTY, Bill. *With shame remembered*. Cassell, 1962.
BERGMAN, G. F. J. and LEVI, J. S. *Australian Genesis: Jewish convicts and settlers 1788–1850*. Adelaide: Rigby, 1974.
BOWES, Smyth Arthur. *The journal of Arthur Bowes Smyth, surgeon, Lady Penrhyn 1787–1789*. Sydney: Australian Documents Library, 1979.
CALEY, George. *Reflections on the colony of New South Wales*. Edited by J. E. B. Currey. Lansdowne, 1966.
CHAPMAN, Don. *1788: the people of the First Fleet*. Cassell, 1981.
CHARLWOOD, Don. *The long farewell: settlers under sail*. Allen Lane, 1981.
CLACY, Mrs Charles. *A lady's visit to the gold diggings*. Lansdowne, 1963.
COBLEY, John. *Sydney Cove 1788*. London: Hodder & Stoughton, 1962.
Sydney Cove 1789–1790. Sydney: Angus & Robertson, 1963.
Sydney Cove 1791–1792. Sydney: Angus & Robertson, 1963.
The crimes of the First Fleet. Angus & Robertson, 1970.
COBBOLD, Rev. R. *The history of Margaret Catchpole*. London, 1846.
CUMES, J. W. C. *Their chastity was not too rigid*. Melbourne: Longman, 1979.
CUNNINGHAM, Peter R. N. *Two years in New South Wales*. 2 vols. Reprint of 1827 English ed. Adelaide: Libraries Board of South Australia, 1966.
CLARK, Lt. Ralph. *The journal and letters of Lt. Ralph Clark*. Sydney: Australian Documents Library, 1981.
CLARK, C. M. H. *A history of Australia*. vol. 1. Melbourne: Melbourne University Press, 1962.
A history of Australia. vol. 2. Melbourne: Melbourne University Press, 1968.
A history of Australia. vol. 3. Melbourne: Melbourne University Press, 1973.
DALY, Harriet. *Digging, squatting and pioneering*. London, 1887.
DE VRIES-EVANS, Susanna. *Pioneer women, pioneer land*. Sydney: Angus & Robertson, 1987.
ELDERSHAW, Flora (ed.). *The peaceful army: a memorial to the pioneer women of Australia 1788–1938*. Sydney, 1938.
FITZPATRICK, Kathleen. *Sir John Franklin in Tasmania*. Melbourne: Melbourne University Press, 1949.
FLETCHER, Marion. *Costume in Australia 1788–1901*. Oxford University Press, 1984.
FREELAND, J. M. *The Australian pub*. Melbourne: Sun Books, 1977.
HASLUCK, Alexandra. *Portrait with background*. Oxford University Press, 1955.
HENEY, Helen. *Australia's founding mothers*. Melbourne: Thomas Nelson, 1978.
HENNING, Annie and HENNING, Amy. *The sea journals of Annie and Amy Henning*. Edited by Joan Thomas. Halstead Press, 1984.

HENNING, Rachel. *The letters of Rachel Henning.* Sydney: Bulletin Newspaper Company, 1952.

HUGHES, Robert. *The fatal shore.* London: Collins Harvill, 1987.

INGLETON, Geoffrey C. *True patriots all: a collection of broadsides.* Sydney: Angus & Robertson, 1952.

IRVINE, Nance. *Mary Reibey—Molly Incognita.* Library Australian History, 1982.

KERR, Joan and FALKUS, Hugh. *From Sydney cove to Duntroon: a family album.* Hutchinson, 1982.

KIDDLE, Margaret. *Caroline Chisholm.* Melbourne: Melbourne University Press, 1950.

KING, Hazel. *Elizabeth Macarthur and her world.* Sydney: Sydney University Press, 1980.

KING, Philip Gidley. *The journal of Philip Gidley King, Lieutenant R.N. 1788–1790.* Sydney: Australian Documents Library, 1980.

MACARTHUR, Onslow S. M. *Some early records of the Macarthurs of Camden.* Reissue of 1914 edition. Adelaide: Rigby, 1973.

MCCONNEL, Mary. *Memories of days long gone by.* London, 1905.

MACKANESS, George. *Australian historical monographs.* Sydney, 1951.

MCLACHLAN, Noel. (ed.). *The memoirs of James Hardy Vaux.* Heinemann, 1964.

MEREDITH, Louisa Anne. *Notes and sketches of New South Wales 1844.* Sydney: Ure Smith in association with the National Trust, 1973.

NICOL, John. *Life and adventures of John Nicol, mariner.* London, 1822.

PHILLIP, Arthur. *The voyage of Governor Phillip to Botany Bay.* London, 1789.

POWNALL, Eve. *Mary of Maranoa.* Sydney: F. H. Johnston, 1959.

ROBINSON, Portia. *The hatch and brood of time.* vol. 1. Oxford University Press, 1985.

SALT, Annette. *The outcast women.* (Macquarie colonial papers.) Hale and Iremonger, 1984.

SHANN, E. O. G. *Cattle chosen.* Perth: University of Western Australia Press, 1978.

SMITH, Robin. *The birth of Australia.* Adelaide: Rigby, John Currey O'Neill, 1978.